THINGS UNSAID

T0293919

POETRY BY TONY CONNOR

With Love Somehow   1962
Lodgers   1965
Kon in Springtime   1968
In the Happy Valley   1971
The Memoirs of Uncle Harry   1974
New and Selected Poems   1982
Spirits of the Place   1986
Metamorphic Adventures   1996

Tony Connor
Things Unsaid

SELECTED POEMS
1960–2005

ANVIL PRESS POETRY

Published in 2006
by Anvil Press Poetry Ltd
Neptune House 70 Royal Hill London SE10 8RF
www.anvilpresspoetry.com

This book is published with financial assistance
from Arts Council England

Designed and set in Monotype Bembo by Anvil
Printed in Great Britain at
Alden Press Ltd, Oxford and Northampton

ISBN 0 85646 385 X

A catalogue record for this book
is available from the British Library

Contents

3   From *Kon in Springtime* (1968)

4   From *In the Happy Valley* (1971)

5   From *New and Selected Poems* (1982)

7   From *Metamorphic Adventures* (1996)

8 *Poems 1996–2005*

Preface

From 1955 to the present I have composed the majority of my poems in what might be termed the "quasi–autobiographical" mode. Such poems are well represented in this selection. Not so the poems composed in less amenable modes, most of which belong to sequences I am unwilling to print in part, i.e. "Seven Last Poems from the Memoirs of Uncle Harry"; "Twelve Secret Poems"; "The Memoirs of Uncle Harry" and "Some Metamorphic Adventures".

However, with misgivings, I have torn a few poems from the body of the last-named sequence; these must suffice to suggest the more devious of my poetic activities.

TONY CONNOR

I

from *With Love Somehow*
(1962)

End of the World

The world's end came as a small dot
at the end of a sentence. Everyone died
without ado, and nobody cried
enough to show the measure of it.

God said, "I do not love you," quite
quietly, but with a final note.
It seemed the words caught in his throat,
or else he stifled a yawn as the trite

phrase escaped his dust-enlivening lips.
At least there was no argument,
no softening tact, no lover's cant,
but sudden vacuum, total eclipse

of sense and meaning. The world had gone
and everything on it, except the lives
all of us had to live: the wives,
children, clocks which ticked on,

unpaid bills, enormous power-blocks
chock-full of arms demanding peace,
and the prayerful in a state of grace
pouncing on bread and wine like hawks.

A Rather Public Statement

I do not intend to contribute
a single line, any half-heard
snatch of mystery
to the street's chronicle.
I am deaf among men,
I am dumb among women,
I am the prince of never-there,
the master of winter.

I have no knowledge to offer
about the marriage bed,
nor am I able to say
where, or why important
decisions were made
affecting the lives
of all who heard them
and many more who did not.

I will not pretend an ability
to judge character from faces;
darkness frightens me
and I am apprehensive in sunlight.
Nevertheless,
mine was the bland smile,
the fur coat of incomprehension
in the catastrophe.

When the trek ended, frustrated
by the abattoir wall,
and the disgusted others
started rewinding the string,
I was in the chip shop
ordering fourpenn'orth.
I had not come all that way
for nothing.

On certain nights I have discerned
complicated patterns
in smudged penumbras
but have never missed my supper.
The voices from alleys
– loving or hating –
I have accepted as part
of a wholesome definition.

You will appreciate my reluctance
to give you directions:
my inability to reach
the homes of others
is widely known –
although one of my hobbies
is studying maps
in the front room.

Finally, let me assure those
who imagine my lending a willing ear,
that my lopsided appearance
is congenital,
and should not be interpreted
as a leaning
towards anything
other than the ground.

Mrs Root

Busybody, nosey-parker,
lacking the vast discretion of most
was this woman. The self-cast
chief mourner at funerals, worker
at weddings, she could sniff out death
in a doctor's optimism, joggle
a maiden's mind (button-holed on the front path)
till virginity bit like filed teeth.

Prepared, without discrimination,
friend and enemy for the grave:
washed and talcumed them all. This woman,
who wore such ceremonies like a glove,
could console a grief-struck household
that hardly knew her name, and then
collect money for a wreath fit to wield
at a Queen's passing. Death-skilled

but no less wedding-wise,
her hand stitched the perfecting dart
in bridal satin. She brought report
of cars arriving, clear skies
towards the church. They were her tears
(pew-stifled) from which the happiest
laughter billowed confetti outside the church doors.
Of best wishes, loudest were hers.

And nobody thanked her. Why doesn't
she mind her own business? they said –
who'd leant upon her. Crude and peasant-like
her interest in brides and the dead.
I thought so too, yet still was loath
to add my voice, sensing that
my secret poems were like her actions: both
pried into love and savoured death.

Autumn

October's cache receives Summer.
Under creaking branches bared to rain
wet wads of leaves clog the gutter.
The chimney-breast darkens with a stain

no fire can dry. Evening mists smother
whatever I saw clearly last week:
the street's end, a faithful lover,
where I am going, words to speak

which mean the same in all weathers.
A general death enters the head
through aches that seem to augur fevers,
and muffled dreams in a heaped bed

there's no warming. Reduced to lumber,
the mind's big sun, ease of sense,
are scoured out, as though in a manner
they were the disastrous trappings of innocence,

known for deception, and thrown over.
What is bad bids to be worse,
and nothing to do but crouch and shudder
over the gaping, rifled purse

you trusted with riches, in a corner
burrowed from slashing wet, harsh gust,
while all through the house smug phantoms mutter
of times too severe for them to outlast.

St Mark's, Cheetham Hill

Designed to dominate the district –
God being nothing if not large
and stern, melancholic from man's fall
(like Victoria widowed early) –
the church, its yard, were raised on a plateau
six feet above the surrounding green.
There weren't many houses then; Manchester
was a good walk away. I've seen
faded photographs: the church standing
amid strolling gentry, as though
ready to sail for the Empire's farthest parts –
the Union Jack at the tower's masthead
enough to quell upstart foreigners and natives.
But those were the early days. The city
began to gollop profits, burst
outward on all sides. Soon,
miles of the cheapest brick swaddled landmarks –
the church one. Chimes, that had used to wake
workers in Whitefield, died in near streets.

From our house (a part of the parish)
St Mark's is a turn right, a turn left,
and straight down Coke Street past the "Horseshoe".
The raised graveyard – full these many years –
overlooks the junction of five streets:
pollarded plane trees round its edge,
the railings gone to help fight Hitler.
Adam Murray of New Galloway
"who much improved the spinning mule"
needs but a step from his tomb to peer in
at somebody's glittering television.
Harriet Pratt, "a native of Derby",
might sate her judgement-hunger with chips
were she to rise and walk twenty yards.

The houses are that close. The church,
begrimed, an ugly irregular box
squatting above those who once filled it
with faith and praise, looks smaller now
than in those old pictures. Subdued
by a raincoat factory's bulk, the Kosher
Slaughter House next door, its dignity
is rare weddings, the Co-op hearse,
and hired cars full of elderly mourners.

The congregations are tiny nowadays,
few folk could tell you whether it's "High" or "Low".
The vicar's name, the times of services,
is specialized knowledge. And fear has gone:
the damp, psalmed, God of my childhood has gone.
Perhaps a boy delivering papers
in winter darkness before the birds awake
keeps to Chapel Street's far side, for fear
some corpse interred at his ankle's depth
might shove a hand through the crumbling wall
and grab him in passing; but not for fear
of black religion – the blurred bulk
of God in drizzle and dirty mist,
or hooded with snow on his white throne
watching the sparrow fall.
                              Now, the graveyard –
its elegant wrought-ironwork wrenched,
carted away; its rhymed epitaphs,
urns of stone and ingenious scrolls
chipped, tumbled, masked by weeds –
is used as a playground. Shouting children
Tiggy between the tombs.
                              On Saturdays
I walk there sometimes – through the drift
of jazz from open doors, the tide
of frying fish, and the groups of women
gossiping on their brushes – to see the church,

its God decamped, or dead, or daft
to all but the shrill hosannas of children
whose prayers are laughter, playing such parts
in rowdy games you'd think it built
for no greater purpose, think its past
one long term of imprisonment.

Little survives Authority's cant
but the forgotten, the written-off,
and the misunderstood. The Methodist chapel's
been bought by the Jews for a synagogue;
Ukrainian Catholics have the Wesleyan's
sturdy structure built to outlast Rome –
and men of the district say St Mark's
is part of a clearance area. Soon
it will be down as low as rubble
from every house that squeezed it round,
to bed a motorway and a new estate.
Or worse: repainted, pointed, primmed –
as becomes a unit in town-planners'
clever dreams of a healthy community –
will prosper in dignity and difference,
the gardened centre of new horizons.

Rather than this I'd see a ruin,
and picture the final splendours of decay:
Opposing gangs in wild "Relievo",
rushing down aisles and dusty pews
at which the houses look straight in
past broken wall; and late-night drunkards
stumbling their usual short-cut home
across uneven eulogies, fumbling
difficult flies to pour discomfort out
in comfortable shadows, in a nave
they praise with founts, and moonlit blooms of steam.

Invasion of the House

Thin in the ear as a bat's squeak,
    and through the house all night like bats swarming,
    dodging and darting from room to room –
a piped pattern upon the dark hours –
    is the laughter, the moan, the disturbed talk
of all the household gods. The flowers

loll on the landing. From her bed
    the mother of many men (seventy years –
    and thirty of them widowed – bleared
to whistling breath and no voice) raises
    a hand in the face of the crowding dead,
summoning sons that have never known her praises

to lean to her mouth from the world's end
    that, if there's strength enough, she may revile
    each and every one: the cruel
issue of love. Young stay-at-home awakes
    suddenly at the pushed sheets' small sound;
chair-cramp forgotten, his headache

in someone else's skull where shrill
    laughter and howls of grief and busy chatter
    swoop from the rafters' gloom, then scatter.
His mother lies, fists clenched, face set
    to a fierce stare, as if in death her will
survived, like the growth of grey beneath her hair-net.

Kingdoms away, in the next room,
    awkwardly swagged and heavy with chirruping dreams,
    his young wife sleeps, her moist palms
against her belly's hump, wherein there stirs
    the son eager to quit the womb,
and get at her breasts, and share this house of hers.

Elegy for Alfred Hubbard

Hubbard is dead, the old plumber:
who will mend our burst pipes now,
the tap that has dripped all the summer,
testing the sink's overflow?

No other like him. Young men with knowledge
of new techniques and theories from books
may better his work, straight from college,
but who will challenge his squint-eyed looks

in kitchen, bathroom, under floorboards,
rules of thumb which were often wrong;
seek as erringly stopcocks in cupboards,
or make a job last half as long?

He was a man who knew the ginnels,
alleyways, streets – the whole district:
family secrets, minor annals,
time-honoured fictions fused to fact.

Seventy years of gossip muttered
under his cap, his tufty thatch,
so that his talk was slow and clotted,
hard to follow, and too much.

As though nothing fell, none vanished,
and time were the maze of Cheetham Hill,
in which the dead – with jobs unfinished
waited to hear him ring the bell.

For much he never got round to doing,
but meant to, when weather bucked up,
or worsened, or when his pipe was drawing,
or when he'd finished this cup.

I thought time, he forgot so often,
had forgotten him; but here's Death's pomp
over his house, and by the coffin
the son who will inherit his blowlamp,

tools, workshop, cart, and cornet
(pride of Cheetham Prize Brass Band),
and there's his mourning widow, Janet,
stood at the gate he'd promised to mend.

Soon he will make his final journey:
shaved and silent, strangely trim,
with never a pause to talk to any-
body: how arrow-like, for him!

In St Mark's Church, whose dismal tower
he pointed and painted when a lad,
they will sing his praises amidst flowers
while, somewhere, a cellar starts to flood,

and the housewife banging his front-door knocker
is not surprised to find him gone,
and runs for Thwaite, who's a better worker,
and sticks at a job until it's done.

1957

At the Plumber's

"She was a cleanly woman,"
Mr Hubbard said, and his eye –
the good one – spilled a tear down
his cheek and into the grey
stubble where he hadn't shaved.

"She didn't let t'doctor know
for ages. She might have lived
if they'd caught it earlier,
but, y'see, the lass was grieved
at finding her underwear
befouled, and kept the secret:
it were pride, really, not fear."

The kitchen clock let loose sweet
chimes for the last half-hour back.
He poked the fire, and spat
into the unruly smoke,
while his bad eye's wobbling glance
flickered over me, and took
off across the room.
                              "Now, since
her passing, I get nowt done,"
he said. "I sit like a dunce
here in this kitchen. Clock's gone
on the blink, there's summat wrong
wi' the chimney flue, and yon
hot-water tank needs mending,
but I 'aven't got the heart. ..."

The kettle started to sing
in the scullery. He sat
with head bent, and scarred hands locked
across his flux-stained waistcoat.

"Still," he said, "the missus joked
to the end with her nurses:
she lost, but wouldn't be licked –
Wot about that tea!"
                                        He rose,
tried again to poke flame
from black coals and red ashes,
and went off into the steam-
filled scullery.
                                What *I* said
would sound formal, and tiresome.
I had returned from abroad
to the street where I grew up,
expecting to find him dead
(having given the death shape
years since in an elegy –
and dressed Janet in black crepe!),
yet here he was, brewing tea:
the survivor of loss, grief,
and prophetic poetry.

1977

Bank Holiday

Bright eyes in a pile of lumber
watching the spanking miles unroll
a seaside day in easy summer
    enter running or not at all
to the bodies without number
whoop of children swoop of gulls
    A lively tune on a tin whistle.

Blazing noon on a metal tangle
see the fat lady's skeleton mate,
Come and Get It, I'm No Angel,
    Kiss Me Quick Before It's Too Late;
Oh the bright and battering sandal
on the concrete's waste of heat
    Enter running or not at all.

Sandy mythologies by the mister
dribble nose and fly blown loose,
flags' and hands' heroic gestures;
    an old hat filling with booze
while the roaring roller coaster
flees its maze above the nudes
    Kiss me quick before it's too late.

Candy floss sticks, syrup waffles,
secret rides in the River Caves,
Scenes of the Harem, Sights Unlawful;
    widows and hucksters thick as thieves
and the day tilts at the bottle
and the starstruck girls believe.
    An old hat filling with booze.

Take me an air trip round the Tower
where, all glorious within,
spangles of the dancing floor
    shake a big bellyful of din
and balloons in splendid shower
fall to zips and hearts undone
    Widows and hucksters thick as thieves.

Rotherham Stockport Salford Nelson
Sheffield Burnley Bradford Shaw
roll by a shining Cinderella
    into the night's enormous maw,
smashin girl and luvly fella
tip the wink and close the door.
    Shake a big bellyful of din.

Sodden straws and french letters,
trodden ices, orange hulls,
clotted beach and crowded gutters.
    A lively tune on a tin whistle
sings to the sea "What matters … matters"
and the street sweepers and the gulls,
    Into the night's enormous maw.

The Burglary

It's two o'clock now; somebody's pausing in the street
to turn up his collar. The night's black: distraught
with chimney-toppling wind and harsh rain –
see, the wet's soaking in on the end gable,
and the frothing torrent, overspilling the broken drain,

accosts the pavement with incoherent babble.
There is the house we want: how easy to burgle,
with its dark trees, and the lawn set back from the road.
The owners will be in bed now – the old couple;
you've got the position of the safe? – Yes, I know the code.

The cock's going mad up there on the church steeple,
the wind's enormous – will it ever stifle;
still, its noise and the rain's are with us, I daresay:
they'll cover what we make, if we go careful
round by the greenhouse and in at the back way.

Here's the broken sash I mentioned – no need to be fearful.
Watch how I do it, these fingers are facile
with the practice I've had on worse nights than this.
I tell you, the whole thing's going to be a doddle:
the way I've got it worked out, we can't miss.

Although, God knows, most things turn out a muddle,
and it only confuses more to look for a moral.
Wherever I've been the wind and the rain's blown –
I've done my best to hang on as they tried to whittle
the name from the action, the flesh away from the bone,

but I think, sometimes, I'm fighting a losing battle.
So many bad nights, so many strange homes to burgle,
and every job done with a mate I don't know –
oh, you're all right: I don't mean to be personal,
but when the day breaks you'll have your orders, and go.

Then the next time the foul weather howls in the ginnel,
when the slates slide, the brimming gutters gurgle,
there'll be another lad I've never seen before,
with the rest of the knowledge that makes the job possible
as I ease up a window or skeleton-key a door.

Still, it's my only life, and I've no quarrel
with the boss's methods – apart from the odd quibble
about allowances and fair rates of pay,
or the difficult routes I often have to travel,
or the fact that I never get a holiday.

Most of the time, though, I'm glad of mere survival,
even at the stormiest hour of the darkest vigil.
... Here's the hall door; under the stairs, you said?
This one's easy because the old folk are feeble,
and lie in their curtained room sleeping like the dead.

Sometimes, believe me, it's a lot more trouble,
when you've got to be silent, and move as though through treacle.
Now hold your breath while I let these tumblers click ...
I've done these many a time ... a well-known model ...
one more turn now ... Yes, that does the trick.

Nothing inside? The same recurrent muddle!
I think the most careful plan's a bloody marvel
if it plays you true, if nothing at all goes wrong.
Well, let's be off. We've another place to tackle
under the blown black rain, and the dawn won't be long

when the wind will drop and the rain become a drizzle,
and you'll go your way. Leaving me the bedraggled
remnants of night, that walk within the head
long after the sun-shot gutters cease to trickle,
and I draw my curtains and topple into bed.

The Croft

The croft, shadowed between houses,
blotchy with grass like fading bruises,
had hardly ground to be called croft,
being no more than an unclaimed cleft

in a grubby, once stately, row
of four-window fronts done in stucco.
Shut like a world in a glass ball
this is where childhood befell

whatever it is that's stepped on
into my moving imagination.
Name, purpose, family face,
were vivid daydreams of that place,

where, ear cocked to the sour earth
and the scavenging rats' scratch beneath
in caved cellars, my mind embodied
populous otherwheres to be studied;

a God who, if he cared to come,
might broken-glass-top wall that kingdom,
or (since an old Jew, who retailed fish
there before his shop was demolished)

might sell the burst mattress, the frames
of bike and umbrella, and the bones
buried by dogs, even the mind
that summoned him from the back of the wind.

The real abides; the poem finds it.
By instinct: cat or dog-wit
of sniff and sixth sense, the poem
follows its own secret way home.

Time, that had shored, crumbles. The years,
their accreted populous otherwheres,
vanish, and I alone am left,
I and the poem and the croft

too close for distinction. Rats beneath
scurry and squeak; from his burst mouth
the ever-present God speaks –
innocuous rhetoric of wet kapok.

Apologue

Having a fine new suit,
and no invitations,
I slept in my new suit
hoping to induce
a dream of fair women.

And did indeed: the whole night long,
implored by naked
beauty – pink on white linen –
I struggled to remove
my fine new suit.

At dawn I awoke, blear-eyed,
sweating beneath encumbering rags.

October in Clowes Park

The day dispossessed of light. At four o'clock
in the afternoon, a sulphurous, manufactured
twilight, smudging the scummed lake's far side,
leant on the park. Sounds, muffled –
as if the lolling muck clogged them at the source –
crawled to the ear. A skyed ball thudded
to ground, a swan leathered its wings by the island.
I stood and watched a water-hen arrow
shutting silver across the sooty mat
of the lake's surface – an earl's lake,
though these fifty years the corporation's.
And what is left of the extensive estate
(a few acres of scruffy, flat land
framing this wet sore in the minds of property agents)
a public park. All else is built on.
Through swags of trees poked the bare backsides
of encircling villas, gardening-sheds:
a ring of light making the park dimmer.
Boys and men shouldering long rods –
all licensed fishers, by their open way –
scuffled the cinders past me, heading for home;
but I stayed on – the dispossessed day
held me, turned me towards the ruined Hall.
Pulsing in that yellow, luminous, murk
(a trick of the eye), the bits of broken pillar
built into banks, the last upright wall,
the stalactite-hung split shells of stables,
seemed likely to find a voice – such pent-in grief
and anger! – or perhaps to explode silently
with force greater than any known to progress,
wiping the district, town, kingdom, age,
to darkness far deeper than that which fluffed
now at the neat new urinal's outline,
and heaved and beat behind it in the ruins.

Like a thud in the head, suddenly become memory,
stillness was dumb around me. Scrambling up
a heap of refuse I grabbed at crystalled brick.
Flakes fell from my hand – a gruff tinkle –
no knowledge there of what brought the Hall low,
or concern either. Neither did I care.
Irrecoverably dead, slumped in rank weed
and billowy grass, it mouldered from here to now,
connoting nothing but where my anger stood
and grief enough to pull the sagging smoke
down from the sky, a silent, lethal, swaddling
over the garden I played in as a child,
and over those children – laughter in the branches –
shaking the pear-tree's last sour fruit to ground.

Porto Venere

One midnight, glittering-eyed, in restless silence,
she left our bed, the tower where we were lodged,
and hurried to the sea. The moon was full.
Over the lanterns in the square, the dancing
couples who'd stay till dawn, it swung seaward
through legions of tiny clouds; and she – high-breasted
beside the harbour's fidget of clunking boats –
blanched and burrowed among the shifting shadows,
hearing only the lonely grotto's roar –
like the moon's voice, or the voice of her own blood.

I did not see her go, but dozed heavy
with wine under the wounds of a pallid icon,
and dreamed her body clung so close to mine
spindrift of sweat scattered from huge surges
of muscled battering, undertow sucked back
surfacing faces, thrust, and filled, and killed
everything but the sea's – until she lay
salty and heavy-eyed within my arms,
murmuring: "Love, the waves, the waves were awful.
The moon went in. I thought that I might drown."

A Journal of Bad Times

In Autumn, begin.
                    Uprooting geraniums,
shaking them gently for storage in darkness,
had heard guns crackle in far streets.
In the deepening sky, one evening,
a plane wrote "Freedom" – a vaporous trail
gone before sunset.
                    Beyond the city, mountains
most often hidden. On clear days certain fields,
a pike, glinting glass. Many went that way,
wheels rumbling towards rock.
                              None saw a good end.
The last birds flew late. South, eagerly
when they went. Still, sparrows at my door
importuned for what bread?

Guard against draughts. Bolt the banging door.

Sat late by small oil, a moth, and one moment's silence.
Books helped me, so did other things:
crossword puzzles, meditation.
                    November rain
stained the chimney breast,
at night the wounded groaned beyond the hedge.
The sink froze.
                    All day long the tanks clattered past,
disturbing earth, churning up cobbles.
Not a face I knew. Guns pointing onwards.

Christmas is nothing without a child.

Ghosts again in the front room.
I thought they'd gone for good, but meaning no harm.
Seeking their own echoes, I think.
Their faces in mirrors.

And then …
New men with the first green shoots.
Declarations, manifestoes, promises
in shoddy eccentric type on grey paper.
"There will be public trials …
                              full restitution …"
Dreamed often: four friends dead,
one in exile, one a traitor to some cause.
But could not say the rest.
After the big winds the battle came back;
                              muddled,
beyond the understanding of many.
The snipers stayed longest,
                              and the sky brightened,
imperceptibly, towards summer.
Twigs from laburnum cluttered the front path.
One branch snapped abruptly while I watched,
suggesting more death.

Sharpen the good saw.

Noticed willowherb in unlikely places:
on the roofs of outside privies, in formal gardens.
Dock leaf and dandelion brightened the ruins
beyond my care.
              The cat went out, never came back,
but the strawberries ripened well. This gave pleasure.
In the topmost room the lodger, enfeebled,
scrabbled the quilt, called for a priest,
                              or rabbi.

Only a lay preacher came, and he starved and rambling.

Trim the hedge. Sweep the cellar. Send letters.

One day it was over, or seemed to be.
                              Someone said
a van with a loudspeaker telling good news …

I think someone said that. And near the end
the birds came back, or perhaps they just came out
to see August, with the din of brass bands,
flaunting banners throwing down arms in the street.
How the children shouted!
                              How the women cried!
I smiled in the garden, clutching a dead root,
and the thrush stood on the aerial opposite,
singing! singing!
                    Old friends returned,
drank my new wine.
                         I welcomed them home.

Child's Bouncing Song

Molly Vickers
wets her knickers,
Georgie's father's big and black,
cream on Sunday
milk on Monday,
I'm the cock of all the back.

Tell me who's a
bigger boozer
Mister Baker beats them all,
from his lorry
watch him hurry,
touch the ground and touch the wall.

Who're the gentry
down our entry –
Mrs Smith's got two TVs,
what if her coat
is a fur coat,
all her kids are full of fleas.

Joan loves Harry,
Jack will marry
Edna when they both grow up,
I'll announce it,
bounce bounce bounce it,
our dog Whisker's had a pup.

High and low and
to and fro and
down the street and up the hill,
Mrs Cuthbert's
husband snuffed it,
she got nothing from his will.

Mister, mister
Shirley's sister
won a prize on Blackpool prom,
mam'll smother
our kid brother
when the school inspectors come.

Skip and hopping
I'm off shopping,
Tuesday night it's pie for tea,
please to take this
ball and make this
song of bouncing song for me.

2

from *Lodgers*
(1965)

In Oak Terrace

Old and alone, she sits at nights
nodding before the television.
The house is quiet now. She knits,
rises to put the kettle on,

watches a cowboy's killing, reads
the local Births and Deaths, and falls
asleep at "Growing stockpiles of war-heads."
A world that threatens worse ills

fades. She dreams of a life spent
in the one house: suffers again
poverty, sickness, abandonment,
a child's death, a brother's brain

melting to madness. Seventy years
of common trouble; the kettle sings.
At midnight she says her silly prayers,
and takes her teeth out, and collects her night-things.

Mayor Isaac Watts

Beyond my great-grandfather's bulk
of waistcoat, beard, and arrogant head,
riddle the dumb couplings it took
to raise him up, to fix his blood.

Firm, on a blanched photograph,
face set as though against light's
attrition, he is the last rough
signpost before the track fades out.

The family seeks no farther back:
issued from God Gloucester gentry
is pride-favoured. This is a rock
worth many a longer history

of shifting fortunes. Only mine
the thoughts that pierce the foxy dark
caught in his eyes: that won't have done
until the dubious dead awake

clamouring at his shoulders. Tramp,
didicoy, son and son conceived
at village fête or harvest romp,
the pretty maid the bailiff loved,

until she swelled – let them appear:
fathers who drank winter away,
families that fought tooth and claw,
graceless lumps of Cotswold clay.

Kneaded together, wrenched apart
I'll see them dance: a toppling rote
of clumsy figures, gay and hurt,
then rammed home down death's throat.

For surer than recollected pride,
known quantities, titles that limn
the civil, virtuous and well-shod,
this rabble makes the man I am

labour at poems, seeking in words
a crude power, anonymous
as all the unnumbered heads
that haunt my great-grandfather's eyes.

A Woman Dying

In a room with a wardrobe far too large –
bought at a sale cheap, or handed down –
this careless woman struggled for breath.
Faded oilcloth stopped short of the skirting boards;
beneath her pyjama-top there flowered
the vivid, cancerous sores. She lay with death.

Chrysanthemums in a white bowl
held their tongues, were not telling the name
of whoever had brought them. Now and then
neighbours and friends appeared to be by her side.
Her husband came, spoke, went – so did the pain;
nightdark, daylight, nightdark, and daylight again.

Already nothingness hung like a smell
among the factual furniture. The bare
bulb in its rusty socket rocked
substance away as her younger sister slept.
"Is that burglars?" she said in the small hours,
who had never worried whether the door was locked.

Something was different, something had come in
through fifty-six years of doors left on the latch,
that fed on neglected duties: dust
gathering unswept, meals she'd forgotten to make.
Perhaps it would go if she did her best:
on tiny observances she fretted dully and fussed.

But could not make redress, nor pay
attention enough to keep her sister's face
sharp as her memory of it. Trees
beyond the window waved branches of goodbye,
and then: "What was it the branches waved?"
Question and answer were like as two peas.

And neither mattered. The pain blanked out
everything but a lusting after death,
or youth, or sleep – they looked the same.
Whatever knew friendly flesh was good, was God.
She choked and spat and coughed and tore
down Heaven with moans until the doctor came.

A needle eased the world away.
She did not see the window's curdled shine
grow fronds and flowers which multiplied
all night despite that thrusting, fiery, breath.
At dawn winter went on without her,
while by the bed her sister stood and cried.

Fashionable Poet Reading

He has forgone the razor for a year
to hide from himself his mooning eunuch smile.
His eye – a disease devouring detail –
finds poems in everything. Should he fail
to feed silence to death, he might think himself queer.

Page after page his active verbs perform
their masculine tricks, his syntax bares muscles
in a fighting stance through which the poor blood thrills
a wishful dream of health. He wills
significant scale on nothings, lest his infirm

grasp of the world appal him, and his claim
to deserved fame be openly suspect. Doubt
must still be howled down: sweating, he bellows out
his repertoire. Fat and guilt
begin to dissolve. He shouts. He is glad he came.

The Agents

The flowers are agents of her will.
She has set them out there to stare in
yellowly from the window-sill
while she is sleeping. Petal and stamen

receive my night-long thoughts. Stored
in damp recesses of clustered leaves
they await tomorrow's commanding word,
when they will give her back what grieves

me and makes me glad – my secret gods
and devils. Nothing escapes her knowledge:
no word's unuttered enough, no mood's
fleeting enough, but that the splodge

of tea-stain on the cloth will tell
as she rinses it, the children's shoes –
seemingly careless where they fell –
will whisper her bent head as she ties

them on to little feet. Her agents
are everywhere. I bear to sit
kitchen-bound, under surveillance
all night, only because I judge it

lesser indignity than to dream
adultery with women whom,
for my sake, she has told to mime
transports of secrecy and welcome.

The Smell

The smell hangs about the bedroom,
and can't be got rid of. Open door
and window, the smell will disappear
for a half-hour, then back it comes

as strong as ever. I don't like
it: part of it's me, mixed with powders,
perfumes, lotions, and hair-lacquers
from that loaded dressing-table of hers.

My smell used to be mine: a treat
to savour in a single bed,
a secret with God. Now my sweat,
sex and gases have been compounded

into a woman's property. Now
my smell is something she wears when
she strips herself for love. I
fear it will not be mine again.

An Evening at Home

Sensing a poem about to happen,
two letters demanded to be written.

One to a man about a dog
began clearly and ended vaguely;

the other, to a girl for old times' sake,
overstepped the bounds of propriety. My teeth began to ache.

From a single suspect raw-edged tooth
the pain spread all over my mouth

before I could stop it. Coupled with
rising flatulence, it nearly overcame faith

in my sacred calling. But back I fought
with a concentration of poetic thought

upon my desk. I almost went over
from the chair in which I'd sat to recover –

and would have done had not the lodger knocked
to say that his sink waste-pipe was blocked.

Using the plunger, I began to feel jaded
and disillusioned: something more was needed

than mere poems to right the world.
My hands were numb, I remembered the millions killed

in God's name. I remembered bombs, gas chambers, famine,
    poverty,
and my greying hair. I could not write poetry.

My nose tingled as though it was going to bleed.
I shut my notebook quietly and went to bed.

A Death in the Family

My father died
the spring I was twenty-five. It had been
a dragging winter. The night was cold
when a distant cousin of his we'd never seen
knocked at the door to tell us. We smiled
uncertainly at one another.
Nobody cried,

none of us grieved –
why should we? He'd been absent for too long:
even my mother couldn't find a tear
to mourn him with. She'd grown strong,
hardened against him in the twenty years
since the day he'd gone, saying he'd be back –
and she'd believed

he would be back.
My sister and I couldn't remember
much about him, and what we could
might have been false. I thought I'd clambered
towards his smile on a rumpled bed,
she felt in her hand a shilling he'd given her, but the tales
made us lose track –

tales we'd been told.
We didn't know what was ours or hearsay
so many people he'd called his friends
had stayed around us, whose every memory or stray
comment fed our starved minds.
But we never thought of his coming back,
or growing old.

"Ironic," I said
to my mother that cold spring night –
the visitor gone, ourselves at table –
"that a man can pass from all knowledge and sight
of family for twenty years. Can dissemble
completely, and yet be found out
as soon as dead."

This is the way
we'd talked of him always, as though he were
a case in the papers. Not, I think,
to put him in perspective, but to ensure
that neither self-pity nor the rank
tendrils of guilt choked the life of the household.
Day by day

he receded farther
into the regions of myth – to which,
no doubt, he'd banished us. Images
do not hurt as much as people; such
details as we gathered were appendices
to empty pages. Our only
parent was a mother.

But we were wrong,
my sister and I, – my mother as well:
calling him "John Connor", with no
suggestion she'd ever slept with him at all.
It took his death to rescue him from limbo:
to give again to an abstract evil
a human tongue.

My Father's Walking-Stick

Swindler, con-man, and embezzler
are a few of the roles my father played.
Declared a bankrupt in '32,
he opened a radio shop in my mother's name,
forging her signature to save time and trouble.
She was the only daughter among
a pack of lads – the last at home,
when he met her. She and a widowed mother
in a well-kept house. No wonder his lodger's eye
brightened towards the ageing girl.
Soon my grandma was baking him meat pies,
calling him "Son".
                    It must have seemed
a good arrangement to all concerned: he,
with the urge to procreate that visits
philandering men after years of contraceptives –
but no home-making instinct, found
a home already made; my mother,
fiercely dutiful, thought she could add
a husband to what existed; my grandma
imagined daughter and self provided for.
Perhaps there was love, too. I can't
answer for that – although my mother
even at sixty-nine's a sucker for silver-tongued men.

Snapshots show him in a cap
with a big neb, his arm round her
on a boat to the Isle of Man: both
are smiling three months before my birth.
Later there's one of her in a laughing pose
next to the backyard dustbin. Taken
by him, it looks affectionate – as though
he'd said, as he clicked the shutter: "Let's
have it backwards-road-about tonight."

But my mother's fervent, legal, honesty
must have shocked him. Out of bed
he couldn't persuade her to accept
his improvisations. When angry creditors
and detectives called, she jibbed at saying:
"I'm sorry, he's gone to London on business."
According to their different lights
they let each other down badly. I was five
when he disappeared with a Royal Warrant
out for his arrest. None of us saw
him again, but twenty years on,
incredibly breaking silence, came news
of his distant death.

                     Among his belongings
(the woman he'd lived with had them in a cardboard
grocery box ready for me to claim or reject)
I found a stout walking-stick.
Thinking it apt that, having been
without support from him for so long,
my mother should have something of him
to lean on at last, I carried it home
three hundred miles under my arm.
Her comment was flat, but had an edge
I couldn't name: "Put it in the hall-stand."
There it has stood, unused, to this day.

My Mother's Husband

My mother worries more
as she grows old, about that period
when he was at home. Not that she ever
admits to doubt of her ramrod-
straight honesty's perfect right
to feel outraged at his behaviour,
not that she says there was some wrong
on her side too – no matter how little.
The way her mind turns back
is like a child retracing steps on a dark night,
vainly scrabbling ground for the bright
coin it had gone to purchase sweets with –
unable, even, to find the hole
through which it must have slipped.

Sometimes she makes a joke
of how her conscience settled
all the bills he let go hang
when he disappeared, or of her luck
in picking such a fool
of a man from all the ones she kept
dangling from her little finger.
More often, though, she sees his criminal streak
as author of her tragedy,
unfailingly lumping with it, even now
not daring to consider longer –
his cruel trick
of being different: deliberately
taking the other side, the opposite view
from 'everyone else.' I think of my
serious clashes with her rigid mind:
her closings, with a blind
'You're getting like your father.'

At seventy there are certain new
infinitesimal hints of tone-
changes in the iron mockery
with which she tells of how he'd go
miles to hear a thing called 'Lohengrin,'
and how she's seen him, thick with lather –
foaming from ear to ear –
posturing at the mirror like a loon,
reciting soliloquies by Shakespeare.

To His Wife

Composed of shadows and damp clothing,
the setting you have left
for me to write my poems in
(having yourself taken
to bed), is witness of your deft
devotion to my downfall.
I must be all for you: loving or loathing –

and either a full-time job. You crave
every preoccupation,
detail of thought not being your care
provided you are there.
Surely tonight, of all nights, when passion
has heaved bodily overboard
any suspicions we had that the other gave

less than we gave ourselves, you might
have left me to do my writing
unencumbered by this array –
the evidence of your washday?
Whose very shadows, jutting, butting,
menace my desk and hand –
familiars of your sleep, daring me to write

of anything but you. This token
of servitude then: a poem
made in your image, despite
my wish to spend these night-
hours as though this hearth and home
knew none but me. A state
in which not the slightest whisper of you need ever be spoken.

Waking

The incubus of nightmare is on my chest
squeezing the rib-cage in. What beast
squats on its haunches, face to mine,
waiting for me to wake, and open
eyes like an owl's – so close are his?
I lie sweating eternities
of clouded fears away until,
hearing the milkman ring the bell,
I know the customary world awaits
beyond my darkness. The incubus fits
a sticky finger into my nose
to find out where the nostril goes.
It is my eldest son – no worse –
two years commander of this universe:
an incubus which babbles "Daddy"
over the pouchy, ageing body
which surely should be small as his
is small, and should be racing downstairs
to the kitchen fire, and a huge man
who laughs and laughs and says "Hello, son."

Lodgers

They came with somewhere else in view,
but scrambled to retrieve my ball,
and smiled and told me tales. I grew
within their shadows: Chew, and Nall,
Entwistle, Mounsor, Mitcham, Grey –
masterful men who could not stay.

Some boozed and came in late, and some
kept to their bedrooms every night,
some liked a joke, and some were glum,
and all of them were always right.
Unwitting fathers; how their deep
voices come back to me in sleep!

I hear them mumbling through the wall
nursery prayers and drunken smut.
I see their hairy fingers maul
sandwiches delicately cut.
I smell their smoky suits, their sweat,
salute them all, and own my debt.

They came, they fidgeted, they went.
Able to settle nowhere long,
theirs were the terms of banishment
that clothe the skeleton. Their strong
fathering figures could afford
little beyond their bed and board.

And yet: enough. Each exile's mite
of manhood – noble in its fall –
bestowed upon me helped me write
a name on nothing. Chew, and Nall,
Entwistle, Mounsor, Mitcham, Grey –
masterful men who could not stay.

The Poet's District

My mind runs on and back and round:
routes of my childhood fixed the shape
of thought; I cannot now escape
shadowy entries, streets that wind,
alleys that are often blind.

The games I played on winter nights –
chancing a labyrinth of dark
limbos between the gaslamps – mark
me one who races fears and doubts
with bated breath, whose short cuts

are tumbling trespasses through sad
gardens abandoned by the rich,
whose hints to pursuers, roughly scratched
arrows on brick and cryptic words
only with difficulty deciphered.

Bounded by solitude, and walls,
and brews that peter out on crofts,
concealed corners, sudden shifts
of level, backs that flirt with ginnels,
double round privies, skirt schools –

deviously beneath the close
horizons of houses, through streets
grown nightmare-still, I take thought
towards that final hiding place
where someone crouches with my face

waiting impatient to be found
and freed by a swift, relieving tig.
I am small and fearful. Very big
and quiet, and cold, and unconcerned,
the tricky district of my mind.

Entering the City

The city lies ahead. The vale
is cluttering as the train speeds through.
Hacked woods fall back. The scoop and swell
of cooling towers swing into view.

Acres of clinker, slag-heaps, roads
where lorries rev and tip all night,
railway sidings, broken sheds
brutally bare in arc-light,

summon me to a present far
from Pericles's Athens, Caesar's Rome,
to follow again the river's scar
squirming beneath detergent foam.

I close my book, and rub the glass:
a glance ambiguously dark
entertains briefly scrap-yards, rows
of houses, and a treeless park,

like passing thoughts. Across my head
sundry familiar and strange
denizens of the city tread
vistas I would, and would not, change.

Birth-place and home! The diesel's whine
flattens. Excited and defiled
once more, I heave the window down
and thrust my head out like a child.

Lancashire Winter

The town remembers no such plenty,
under the wind from off the moor.
The labour exchange is nearly empty;
stiletto heels on the Palais floor
move between points of patent leather.
Sheepskin coats keep out the weather.

Commerce and Further Education
won't be frozen. Dully free
in snack bars and classrooms sits the patient
centrally heated peasantry,
receiving Wimpies like the Host;
striving to get That Better Post.

Snow on the streets and Mini Minors
thickens to drifts, and in the square
from dingy plinths, blind eyes, stone collars,
the fathers of revolution stare,
who – against pikes and burning brands –
built the future with bare hands.

The Graveyard

One winter morning, half in a dream,
the young boy lurched from his heaped bed
before the sky hinted at light.
The window, encrusted with frosty flowers,
concealed the tangle of whispering streets
knotted together around the graveyard.

All night long he had dreamed of the graveyard,
and now he recalled it was more than a dream:
it waited for him among the streets.
Oh how he wished to be warm in bed!
He rubbed a hole in the frosty flowers,
saw cold darkness, and switched on the light.

He hated to be out before it was light
delivering papers; and though the graveyard –
its waiting tombs and cobweb flowers –
was what disturbed him and made him dream,
he wouldn't have got from the lumpiest bed
to walk the pleasantest dawn-wet streets

given the choice. And yet the streets
were where he must go. In the acrid light
of the bare bulb he dressed by the bed,
shivering with cold and thoughts of the graveyard.
He tried to forget his horrible dream
of a hand beckoning from grey grave-flowers.

He wished he delivered bread, or flowers –
jobs of the cheerful, daytime streets –
but how could he, at eleven, dream
of saving: "I'll only work when it's light?"
His mother laughed when he spoke of the graveyard;
she said: "It's just that you like your bed!"

He laced his boots and made his bed,
straightening the quilt's misshapen flowers,
and soon he was on his way to the graveyard
by a rambling route that led through streets
dark between pools of feeble gaslight.
He delivered his papers as though in a dream.

It was faintly light when he reached the graveyard.
The streets whispered: "Have you brought flowers
for the dead who dream of you in their narrow beds?"

Alex at Forty

I find him in the spare room,
curled on a mattress on the floor,
another over him. His face
is pouched, he snores amidst the reek of beer.

At ten in the morning, still flat,
with last night's revelry curdled to
a nasty mouth, he opens pig-
eyes on a crumpled suit, a new day.

Blearily to our fire (there's nothing
owing) he comes to make his peace
on stinking feet. My wife is polite
but disapproving. He coughs, he hems and haws,

abject and arrogant by turns.
Apologies twist his mouth like insults:
he laments his squandered gifts, his thirst,
family pride, guilt, and all Celts –

but borrows ten shillings. Half inclined
to hate my job – the monthly cheques
with which I pay the bills, I buy
a poet's share in the dog-rough fall of Alex,

who leaves at eleven: Opening time.
I watch from the window. In the street
his step recovers its jauntiness.
My wife serves coffee, bitter as defeat.

Old Beswick

Always death's companion – bearded,
stooping to earth and mumble-worded
with flower heads, dug-up roots, the hutched
rabbits he fed on crisp lettuce and grass fetched
each day fresh from his nursery garden
he was the terror of my childhood. Forbidden
things lurked in the steam behind his patched
greenhouse glass; both his legs were wooden.

It took years of my growing-up
to cleanse from sleep the bedraggled gap
in a hedge through which, with a mouthful of curses,
he came at me once, his pee-stained baggy trousers
slapping those rigid limbs. A lad
told me all of him was turning into wood –
his own coffin, the kids whispered. Houses
were safe and so were streets: I stayed in and read,

and played amidst the comfort of alleys,
blotting his holy of black holies
out of my mind with hopscotch, tig,
Masterman Ready, errands with basket or jug,
and homework. Never daring to trespass
again in that part of the park where an ivied buttress
leant on the Hall's remaining wall – a sag
and stagger of crystalled brick bounding the monstrous

garden where he, flowers, steam,
rabbits, and death, kept bloodstopping company. Time
plays strange tricks on memory: he married
a young widow, when I was twenty and hadn't worried
or dreamed about him for years. His face,
elderly and benign, smiled from the close
print of the local paper, but my sleep was harried
anew by the old evil, roaring its curse

on all imposture, the open furnaces
of its eyes dazzling the lake, and the houses
beyond the gates, as I ran and ran
away through the years, and on on on
came the wooden legs, lurching the fiery
twilight at every step, till the mouth hairy
and vast as God's cried, "Perish the man
that takes my name in vain," and I woke in a fury

of sweat and sheets, sure that death
for the old man had burst from the pith
of a child's nightmare into the present,
and through the dawn-wet streets hastened
that moment towards his marriage bed.
He lived for years longer. People said,
when he died, that but for arthritic hips there wasn't
a thing wrong with him: what an end for a good

old soul – to slip and fall in the nursery
garden he'd made his life! Wary
of whatever was to disturb, I kept
away for ages. Then, on a day nipped
by autumn's first teeth, returning
from somewhere beyond the park, I smelled leaves burning,
and trod again the familiar path between lopped
columns, fallen corbels, and ironwork turning

wholly to rust in bushy grass.
Silence; and woodsmoke curling across
a waste of weeds. In seeding cabbage
the hutches were random planks. A heap of garbage
rotted amongst the broken pipes
of the caved greenhouse. I wondered what hopes
proved false, as I walked – devoid of fear or courage –
towards the young keeper's fire by the small copse.

3
from *Kon in Springtime*
(1968)

A Child Half-Asleep

Stealthily parting the small-hours silence,
a hardly-embodied figment of his brain
comes down to sit with me
as I work late.
Flat-footed, as though his legs and feet
were still asleep.

He sits on a stool,
staring into the fire,
his dummy dangling.

Fire ignites the small coals of his eyes.
It stares back through the holes
into his head, into the darkness.

I ask what woke him?

"A wolf dreamed me" he says.

Saying It

Questions of tact are uppermost,
even when control appears to be lost.
To develop which, one cultivates silence
as well as words, weighing to the ounce
pauses long and short, awkward searchings,
and constructions that chase themselves in rings
till they peter away in utter defeat.
There may be a notable tact in that.
As in giving an embarrassing amount away,
in "baring the soul" autobiographically,
in being tactless. What is demanded
is that the poet be openhanded
enough to allow his skill to grip
of all possible shapes the one shape
without which the poem would not be there,
chunky or clinking, fleshed from empty air.
It is like a good marriage: the man will know
the true wifely agreement from the say-so.
At times he will sulk, or shout, or practise disgust:
whichever seems to offer the most
likelihood of the hoped-for answer
to the non-questions it is impossible to ask her.
The tact is the keeping of a balance –
if that is what ensures, always, another chance.
Discounting nothing – kitchen trivia, boredom,
and the dreams of escape that make a home.

In the Children's Room

Sometimes when they are asleep,
I stand by the beds looking
at those beautiful variations
of the sadly drooping
flesh on our bones. I long,
on such nights, for mastery

of their futures; as though they
might benefit by magic
of my close care – protected
from the poison and decay
of time, and the stains that mock
clean intention. But the dead,

who haunt my house severely,
raise their loud voices against
such nonsense, and I think of
my own poems: how slowly,
and from what fallings and stains
they have grown; likewise my love.

Then I bend, and smooth back hair
from a hot forehead, or, maybe,
stroke a cheek. Not reconciled
to the undoubted wearing-
out and dirtying they
must suffer to die wise men,

or fools; but less troubled by
the futility of my fierce
prayers, and the proud but modest
gestures of fatherly
love I make as though by force
of habit over each bed.

On the Cliff

Between the scented soap works
and cloud-capped cooling towers,
I walked one summer evening
swishing the soot-stained flowers.

Below, the black river
snaked around the racecourse,
drudging to distant sea
the dregs of commerce,

and huge across my vision
under the streaky sky
from Chapel Reach to Pomona Dock
the changing city lay,

swarming invisibly
with its intricate, restless hordes
of common humanity –
the keepers of the Word.

All I have accepted
to exercise heart and wit:
the unpredictable home
of the ever-unlikely poet.

There on the shifting cliff
where nothing built will stand
(local eruption of a fault
that runs across England)

I watched the lights come on,
and listened to a lover
coaxing a silent girl
under near cover,

and farther off the yells
of children at some chase:
voices much like my own –
the accent of the place.

The accent of the place!
My claim to a shared load
of general circumstance
with the hidden multitude.

Yet strange, despite the wish –
because my chosen task
was the making of poems –
I shivered in the dusk:

aware that my shining city
did not care one jot
for me as its celebrant,
or whether I wrote or not.

I might have been unborn,
or else long dead,
but before I reached my home
I had perfected

the sociable, lonely poet,
a rueful one-man sect,
in an ignorant, ugly city –
his God-given subject.

Flights

As a child I was fortunate
in having the gift of flight.
Many familiar streets and bodies
was I able to view from eight feet
above ground level; many conversations
and quarrels I observed secretly
(being invisible).
I did not think it unusual.

Youth crippled the gift somewhat.
Only on certain nights
in cold, unpleasant dreams,
housebound and lapped by evil
airs and murmurings, did I float
like a grotesque balloon
over snoring sleepers,
and down draughty, threadbare stairs.

By eighteen I could not rise at all,
but – as though in compensation –
dead relatives, and earlier
occupants of the house
began to make themselves known to me.
The unloved – an asthmatic aunt,
two weeping second cousins,
a bearded suicide, and a baby

that choked on a boiled sweet –
all made importunate demands
I lacked the experience to
satisfy, or even to understand.
When I started writing poems
they stopped visiting me,
except for Uncle Harry
who insisted that he was my guide,

and under this pretext
succeeded in writing the memoirs
he had been revolving in his head
for twenty-five years
in the County Mental Hospital.
He was a man with eyes
like the winter sun's reflection
in two dust-laden windows;

I was glad to see him gone.
In mid-life I neither fly
nor receive the frustrated dead.
The days are women's baking smells,
and the demanding cries of children.
The nights, when they are broken,
are broken by flesh, and the sleepy moans
of my children learning to master flight.

Considering Junk

It lies there, vivid in its dereliction,
among fine ashes from combustion stoves,
drippings of tinned tomatoes
that smelled peculiar, soiled disposable
nappies, and other household grot.

Having exhausted, or frustrated expectation,
it emanates a certain smugness –
if you are of such a mind to think so.

A painter might take away the slither
of red polythene down a scorched bucket
into the crumbly texture of old flock
beneath, a sculptor (to the point of plundering)
broken bannister-ends like totems
to an ultimate, perfect, mass beyond masses.

You may look at it in different ways …

There are, for instance, certainly, numerous
homilies here for the religious man
with a touch of the poet.
                              As for the poet
himself: in this rigorous age he is wary of metaphor,
far more of symbol, and if he is the householder
(as I am) whose annual clear-out
has overflowed dustbin, grocery boxes,
and mildewed split trunk, onto
the garden path, his dreams alone are likely
to dwell on things he threw away.
                              Cumbersome, brokendown
junk talking all night with the eloquence of poems.

Above Penmaenmawr

The upland farmers have all gone;
the lane they laid twists without purpose,
visiting broken gates and overgrown
gardens, to end in clumps of gorse.

Their unroofed houses, and fallen barns,
rich in nettles, lie dead in hiding
from the wind that howls off Talyfan's
saw-tooth ridge; their walls divide

bracken from bracken; their little church
of bare rock has outlasted use:
hikers' signatures in the porch,
"Keys obtainable at the Guesthouse".

Yet, not to sentimentalize,
their faces turned from drudgery
when the chance showed itself. There is
hardly a sign of the husbandry

of even the last to leave – so slight
was their acceptance by the land.
They left for the seaside towns, to get
easier jobs, and cash in hand.

Five miles of uplands, and beyond –
a thousand feet below – the coast,
its bright lights twinkling; freezing wind
dragging the cloud down like a frost

from Talyfan. Alone upon
these darkening, silent heights, my fears
stay stubbornly with the farmers, gone
after six hundred thankless years.

The Globe Inn

I think of Dolly, last one at the feast:
picker of scraps from a bony carcase.
Three hundred years declined to this –
tradition living on as a deformed ghost
in the mind of an idiot.
                                        The almost human
face drifting about the house,
mottled and round like the moon's face,
or bent over boiling chutney, through steam looming,
returns as an image overlaying the sign
of the globe from which continents had faded.
Sister, no more than a business head –
as alien as her long negotiation
to sell the place to a big brewery. The Severn
at the door, the water meadows,
the cathedral rising clear of the shadows
of Gloucester's ancient roofs – "a rural heaven
whose profits could be doubled if modernized."

But Dolly with her fifteen tin
"wedding rings", her "marriages" to fishermen,
and mongoloid smile, had nicknames for bird, beast,
and flower, saw the scattered family dying
in England's dirty cities.
                                        "Flo
fell in the kitchen dead, I saw
while I was asleep."
                                        "Sarah is sick and going
to die, I spoke to her yesterday."
                                        "Uncle Jack
has gone to Heaven."

                    Already the car-
trade gave the best returns. Sister
haggled about Goodwill with a man in black –
the brewery's representative – but died before
she could clinch the deal. Dolly saw
that coming, too, and whimpered in fear,
dreaming beside her glass beads and her teddy bear.

They put her in a Home. Sister willed
the Globe to the friend she'd not quite wed
because of Dolly: good, faithful, Jud
who'd helped in the bar for years. He sold
as quickly as he could. Dolly fell down
a flight of stairs and broke her neck;
the Matron stated she had been homesick.

My mother said: "Well, that's the old place gone,
your grandma would have wept; she always thought
it was ours by rights." And then: "Poor Dolly.
I remember her as a child: poor Dolly."

The end of a history; our last connection cut
with three hundred years of England. Never again
would Sister send us "conscience money",
boxes of elvers – wet spaghetti
we tipped down the whiter pan and pulled the chain.

The Gamekeeper's Dotage

When he was eighty-two they opened
the first of the Supermarkets
on the main road. I don't think
he even noticed the mighty pyramids
of tins and washing-up liquid
at cut prices piled in the window –
although one Sunday morning
he caught in bare hands
the panful of boiling peas
that tipped from his black hob.
The house was silent and dirty;
it stank as if death were there already;
you couldn't be sure in rooms
where you peered as though through water
that hadn't been changed for years.
Of course, you never stayed long (the stench,
the dinginess, the look that showed –
again – he didn't know who you were),
hut let him for his pride's sake brew
a pot of tea, and mumble for a while
among his towering memories, which
towards the end came down to one.

It was troubling to visit him by then;
to step from the main road's redevelopment,
the loaded shopping-bags, the lines
of shining cars, into that hush
where over and over he lifted arms
like trembling sticks, pulled the trigger,
and killed it for the Duke – the last
stag on the great estate
that has been a public park for fifty years.

Kon in Springtime

The Russian landlord who lets next door's
once carefully cared-for rooms to any-
body, is angry about the money
that's gone from his desk. He doesn't mind whores,
or coloured students, or jailbirds,
or kids. He trails to the 'bins in a tatty
dressing-gown – up at seven-thirty,
shaking his aristocratic head

at the evil in men. I like sharing
the area with him: revolutions,
pogroms, years in a concentration
camp, haven't made him despair
of human nature. He won't call the police
(he never does), or tell the suspect
to get his paper-baggage packed –
and he *isn't* liberal-minded. He'll curse

rotten the dirty bastard who
robbed him, and make life unpleasant,
deliberately, for all his tenants
for at least a day, and perhaps two.
But can't keep it up – he carries his years
gaily: the bow-tie, and the collar
of astrakhan are popular
sights in every local bar,

and at sixty-three, it's said, he still
has charm to enjoy the guarded virtue
of good wives, who open their legs to
nothing else that isn't legal.
May I survive a barbarous age
as well! Muttering, and miming punches,
under a clear blue sky he crunches
back to the door across the spillage

of cinders from his pail. I watch
from the kitchen table, where I've sat
all night, struggling to be a poet
in mid-journey at masterful stretch
among the rich imperatives
of family life. The Russian pauses,
staring at me as though my house is
haunted – reluctant to believe

I'm up at such an hour. He comes
worriedly to my window, certain
I must be awake because of children:
"Is it bad-sick, your little ones?"
he asks. I reassure him, they
vomited, but are asleep again.
He beams – who has never heard of Pushkin –
and says "It will be a lovely day."

4
from *In the Happy Valley*
(1971)

New Place

Muffling our gasps of lust
trucks without mufflers
shift gear on Route 9.

Their headlights sweep the room;
we are two thrashing
ghosts as they rend past
going somewhere as fast
as the country road
will allow.
         We lie back,
going nowhere, waiting
in dense black
for the next truck's passing.
Our foreign white flesh
on the all-American
maplewood floor resists
every parable I begin.
In the approaching roar
shadows shape and lengthen.

Here there are new rules
to be learned. We appear
disappear, appear, as the night cools.

Good Times

There are days when the world
welcomes you in.

The landscape lies open;
the people, noticing
and unnoticing of you,
are alike in making you known.

A curse has been lifted, you could believe;
momentarily, it is true, in the scale of things –
but lifted.
    You go about happy but puzzled
                              naked–chilled
smiling into the voracious laughter of your youngest child.

Walking by Birchwoods

The moon like a slippery secret
comes clear of the humped hills.

I am returning from the laundromat
thinking about the dead,
as though that watched turbulence of cleansing
had dislodged discreet spirits.

The least of them knows me too well;
some of them are my spitting image
and kick the snowbanks as I do,
whistling the latest tunes through clenched teeth.

Not that they come to accuse;
merely to remind in Massachusetts.

My old amiable companions!
Insulted, hurt, ignored — no matter,
they are glad to see me doing so well:
for whom else did they die?

My burden is children's clothes in pillowcases.

See those shimmering shapes dismember
at the first car's headlights!
Into the dark wood they scurry:
dried snow blown by the night wind.

The moon follows me mildly down the valley.

In the Locker Room

Everything's clean and jolly:
genitals, butt, and belly
show with a nakedness
that causes none distress.
Between the locker rows
heaps of abandoned clothes
lie like a beaten race
crumpled in its disgrace.
All's cheer above – the Lords
of muscle-power and words
tingling from gym and joke
relax for a quick smoke.
Glad to be back again
in this clear world of men
I banish from my mind
the dark thoughts of its kind.
I rub my itching balls:
the seed of criminals
and maniacs waits
in those hanging fruits.

Flu at the Sheraton Chicago

Channels of smudgy faces
ride upon the one unvarying voice:

Bad breath bad guys deodorants and death.

The bulk-bought furniture,
the personalized paintings, the selection of magazines
in the rack lie stunned in the room's heat.

If I force the venetian blinds
in a sudden panic, I will sense through aimless dense
snow the real world:
                     Metropolis where the judgements
of commerce take grey desirable shape.

Out in the dark
the Great polluted Lake crackles its icy fringe.
Slender white horizontals thicken upon the skeleton
of the tallest apartment block in the world.

My pill is like a parody of the bright spot:
the last embarrassed girl and the last corpse
being flushed away.
                  I gulp it down.

My sleep is haunted by the faithless multitudes of America.

The Attack

Into the mind's emptiness
come thoughts of sickness:
the body, the brain choking –
agony-end of everything.

Consciousness narrows.
The pounding heart's slow blows
assume midnight. The room
throbs like a struck drum.

There is nothing, nothing at all
to be done – the attack is fatal.
Ears whine, nausea drags
sideways, beneath wild legs

the floor shakes; full moon's face
is a doctor, helpless,
watching nerves sever
eyes go out mouth slaver.

Then you are back, complete,
not knowing the half of it,
but magically healed
to a ponderous night-world

of cricket and frog sounds,
far wars and near wounds,
while sundry small thoughts purr
into a certain future.

Something has won something,
for what it is worth. Your strong
being prowls through the house.
The moon is anonymous.

Listening to Bach in Franklin County

The police in the cities prepare for summer,
there is much talk of the need for order.

A fugue in the wilderness
ravishes the hearts of a few impotent men.
With lunatic fastidiousness
the music steps from my window
towards the scrub forest before
and the Shopping Plaza behind,

inviting assassination –
such fervent benevolence open to the night air.

It all happens again:
                    the just go down,
the greedy, the stupid.
                    Battlefields
become the pastures of scholars.

One thinks of ways to preserve one's sanity …
fugues whose structure one only senses,
a political sticker on the windshield
that partly obscures one's vision.

The forfeiture of giant miseries
                                   to write
a small poem at midnight.

Making Love Half-Asleep

Whose hands are these questing
my body? There is a face
I do not know forming
against mine. My arms embrace

flesh and it is demanding
of me – the alien stink
swilling my brain, rending
the dream in which I think

clearly and fast. I squeeze
it dully, and enter it with
fingers that cannot choose,
and I am riding wrath,

stirring the turmoil's centre,
in the furious howl
of the storm I am a splinter
stuck in the blackest bowel

of creation. I am going to be dead,
surely: smothered, fused
with a monster cold-blooded
and lecherous, violent in its crazed

appetites. Afterwards,
lying drained and chilled,
I know what we are; but words
will not serve. I hold

your hand, and we are home
my poor silent companion,
watching ourselves become
man and wife again.

Morning Song

This northerly light is bleak;
bedrooms should face south.
The mirror claws your cheek
like time itself; your mouth

(how often moved to kiss
its image of pretty glass?),
puckered and bloodless,
drops open on "Alas!"

Archaic, tragic, tall,
your strong form gathers in
from a million bedrooms all
the grief of beautiful women.

Every ageing body
outraged by morning light
you don for lonely study –
symbol and anchorite.

And I, a tousled fool –
not meant to understand,
except in poems – recoil
as if from a large demand

I cannot answer, although
you don't so much as glance
towards me and my show
of sleeping ignorance.

My operatic dear,
lost in your noble part –
sombre, nude, bizarre,
no live man's sweetheart –

descend to feed the children:
assume the debased forms
from which flow affection,
abuse, domestic storms,

for these I can well gauge,
and grapple with something more
than frightened patronage
(now pretending to snore).

Names on Stone

In old graveyards
I could wonder what mattered.
All those particular names
affect me like a starry sky.

Who was a good man?
Who cheated many?
Who greeted each day with a song?
Whose life was one long pain?

Tumours, palsies,
hare–lips, hunch–backs
are gone with kindness
and the odour of sanctity.

Some evidence of riches remains,
and of poverty; but both
soon become part
of the same official care.

If you go back far enough
even the most stubborn accumulations
lose all meaning.
Stones hold names

like stars. You look,
and around you
the emptiness deepens
with everything named that no one knows.

An Anonymous Painting

In a tessellated courtyard a young lady
is teaching a dog to beg. A child
plays with a ball. An aged servant
drying her hands on a gathered apron,
looks out smiling upon the scene
from the door of the house. The walls of the courtyard
(mellow red brick, about ten feet high)
are partly obscured by trailing woodbine
of a colour which suggests summer is over.
The light, too, has the glow of withdrawal,
though it dwells with the amplitude of eternity
upon cracks in the tiles, the dog's tongue,
the smooth neck of the lady, and the shoe
peeping from beneath the child's dress.
Above the courtyard the land falls away
in strangely tilted perspective that shows
the buildings, towers and spires of the city
the courtyard is part of, and – beyond – a landscape
where a drunken-looking peasant ambles aimlessly
towards a small copse on a small hill,
and two workers absorbed in their task
lift scythes to standing grain in a field
sprinkled heraldically with neat stooks.
Farther off is a sea, empty of ships,
and farther off still – where the trembling blue
distances curdle into frilly mountains –
comes on, in a descending glitter of highlights,
the minute beginnings of the monstrous army
that will conquer, loot, and sack the city.

5

from *New and Selected Poems*
(1982)

A Short Account at Fifty

I was conceived in the black
of midnight and ignorance.
No more of a true romance
for being out of wedlock.

I fell to earth in a town
smoke-dingy, stinking of wastes.
Echoes of Great War *Last Posts*
reminded me of dead men.

A new war broke out. I crouched
in a shelter underground.
It seemed like the threatened end,
but peace came, drizzling and botched.

Adulthood tugged at my balls:
now I was a Serviceman:
"Army of Occupation"
they called us – boys full of boils.

Demobbed, and back in England,
I slept, ate, worked, went back to bed.
Labouring for small reward:
could such dullness be demeaned?

By degrees I found my heart
was master of prick and pen:
I married and had children,
I sat at a desk and wrote.

Years passed. The blink of an eye
turned my wife into ex-wife.
I shook the marriage-mud off,
and found myself high and dry

in a most unlikely place,
Middletown, Connecticut.
Here I recall, or forget
my various histories.

And dally in middle age
with what frightened me in youth,
dissipating in good faith
a Methodist heritage.

Look for me on a barstool,
or in some kind woman's bed,
talking hard, and undismayed
by folks who think me a fool.

Or see me in the evening
sedate and gravely amused
to find myself once more faced
with a poem on the wing.

Not that the world has improved
as my understanding's cleared:
monstrously base, savage-bored,
it snarls at me to be loved, –

no less than when I was born,
many years and miles away:
the careless, proxy by-blow
of young men killed on the Somme.

Sunday Afternoon: Heaton Hall

for Marjorie Boulton

"They're not *real* cats," my sister
said, her lips pressed to the glass
that separated us from
the tiny, silent kitchen.

"Don't be daft – of course they are!"
I said, lips almost as close.
"They've been killed, and emmed with balm,
and dressed like men and women."

"Ugh!" she said, flouncing away,
"I think it's quite disgusting" –
and catching sight of a school-
friend through the huge bow window,
she ran from the room to play
in the rose-garden, among
the cheerful crowds who would fill
the park until the horn blew
for the closing of the gates
at sundown.
                An attendant
stuck his grey face into mine
and lectured me about noise
as soon as she'd gone. "But it's
not fair!" I said, "It wasn't
me, it was *her* who ran!"

"You're pests, you bloody young boys,
I'd clear out the lot of you
if I had my way," he said.

He gave me a guarded shake,
and hobbled off to caution
a youth who was about to

tap the top of a bronze bead
of Palmerston.
                    This new trick
of my sister's – having fun
and letting me pay the price –
was not one I liked at all.
As I examined the cat-
tableaux in their glass-fronted
scaled-down rooms, I thought of ways
of asserting my rightful
mastery: of proving that
a nearly-ten-year-old lad
could always get the better
of a sister not yet nine;
but the motionless tabbies
and toms, staring sightlessly
at one another over
cups of tea, and games of gin-
rummy and chess, seemed to tease
from my mind its brotherly
ambitions.
                    There were about
twenty cases in all – each
depicting a different
domestic scene. *The Bankrupt*
showed a drawing room, ornate
and richly furnished, in which
a portly, pompous Merchant-
Prince stood tragic and erect
against the fireplace as he
told his wife and small children
of his ruin. The tom's striped
expression somehow conveyed
a world of business worry
above wing-collar, silken
tie and black suit. His wife wiped
a tear from her eye, and tried

to comfort the two kittens
in frilly dresses who knew
that something was wrong, and were
hiding their furry faces
in their paws.
                    Most of the scenes
were happy, though: – the tableau
called *A Party Below Stairs*
made me laugh out loud. The case
was crowded with alley cats
dressed as chambermaids, butlers,
cooks and so on. One lay drunk,
a wine bottle in his paw;
others wore saucepans as hats;
some were dancing the Lancers;
some flirted; some swilled down drink.
In the middle, on a chair,
stood a disreputable
moggy with one eye missing.
He looked like a gypsy, and
was scraping from a fiddle
the silent music that filled
the room.
                    Somewhere a bell rang,
and soon I heard the raw sound
of the horn rasping from hill
to boat lake, to rose-garden,
to landscaped hill.
                    "Now sod off,
sonny," the attendant said.
"We're closing in five minutes,
and if I catch you laughin'
at them exhibits and stuff
again, you'll be blacklisted,
and not let in!"
                    His bright boots
twitched, as though he would have liked

to kick me from the Hall, but
he made do with a fierce glare,
so I stayed with the cats
a moment, before I walked
into the foyer and out
of the enormous front door.

The rose-garden was empty
when I reached it – except
for a cripple with two sticks
plodding towards the far gate.
Then, from the back of a tree,
my sister appeared and slapped
some roses into my fist.

"Hide these under your raincoat,"
she said, "They're for mam."
                                            "You've pinched
them! – You were hiding!" I said.

"I was just having a pee,
Clever!" she said, – "Look: I'm wet."

I punched her and strode off, hunched
over flowers and hatred.

On the bus she said sweetly:
"They weren't *real* cats – what d'y' bet?"

Invalids

Whether the wintergreen smelled
of antimacassars, or
the antimacassars smelled
of wintergreen, I don't know.
Both, I imagine – those rooms
were too small for things to keep
individual presence;
too small and too full of sleep,
and sickness, and silent hours
brooding upon life and death.
From where I sat the pot dogs
stared out from the tarnished glass
on the mantelpiece (the rooms,
my visits, all seem the same),
the flowers on the blanket
drooped in bunches to tangle
with the carpet's threadbare blooms,
and the great sepia stag,
in the sepia forest,
under the sepia sky,
yearned, full of admiration,
for the lion on a field
of Union Jack leaping
colourfully from the lid
of the assorted-biscuit
tin being offered to me
by the old man or woman
smiling on the stacked pillows.

How long had those invalids
been lying in the front rooms
my grandma used to visit,
leaning on me and her stick?
What were they bedridden for?

And who were they – apart
from people she knew? Not one
has a face I remember.
Not a word comes back to me
of the talks about old times
they must have had with grandma,
or the polite enquiries
they probably made of me.
Nothing comes back but the smell
of wintergreen. Every
other detail – (like the lace
runners, the pokerwork plaques,
the fake-marble fire-surrounds,
the gas brackets, brass bedsteads,
bottles of medicine, spoons,
brown bakelite wirelesses
and small change on bedside stands,
that I hadn't intended
to mention) is enlisted
for the sake of this poem –
which might otherwise be vague,
and maunderingly shamefaced
at so many small sickrooms
so thoroughly forgotten.

Grandma and the Blitz

My grandma sat on the bed,
spilling over the edge
like a huge lump of dough.
Her eyes looked already dead,
her mouth dropped long beads of spit
onto her grey nightgown:
one glance and I was off –
sure she was having a fit.
I was only ten, and wrong
about a lot of things:
who Mr Chamberlain
was, why Germans yelled "Achtung!"
how many guns the Spitfire
carried inside each wing;
but I was nearly right
about grandma – the doctor
said she had suffered a stroke.
My mother sent me out
to play, and for three days
hardly bothered me or spoke.
I was glad to be alone –
those were exciting times,
with bombers on their way
and most of the children gone
from the city to seaside
and country. There were air-
raid shelters to explore,
barrage balloons overhead,
a strange anti-aircraft gun
under camouflage nets
in the park, and no school
to interfere with my fun.

Some time after grandma died
the children drifted back
and the city was blitzed.
"Thank goodness your grandma's dead,"
my mother sighed one cold night,
as we crouched in the dark
of the cellar with bombs
exploding to left and right,
"This would have killed her." The past
didn't interest me;
I was impatient for
the "All Clear", and then breakfast,
and then the morning treats:
swastika-marked tail-fins,
and shrapnel and shell-shards
picked from the smoking wet streets.

A Photograph of My Mother with Her Favourite Lodger

Looking at these loved faces –
his above a limp bow tie,
hers beneath a flowered hat –
I try to catch their voices
from thirty-five years ago,
and I can never do it.

Except in dreams, and then I
am a shy uncertain boy
listening amid uproar
to grand sounds of poetry,
while air raid sirens nearby
shriek out a too late Beware.

He is mangling bits of Lear
and the *Rubáiyát*, large hands
sawing the air, gargoyle face
twisted as though on a sour
taste, oblivious to bangs
of guns and bombs, and to us.

She is boiling with disgust:
"The fool's showing off again,
what are you listening for!"
I am his captive, held fast
by a strong incantation
of which he is not aware.

This scene didn't take place
in fact, although he was
our lodger during the war,
and he *did* first come to us
through flattened streets and smashed glass
when the city was on fire.

No: it is my sleeping mind's
gaudy vision of the Child-
hood of The Poet, replete
with frightening figures and
destructive detail. Beguiled
I may have been by the fruit

of that raucous Yorkshire voice,
scarred I certainly was by
my mother's sneering hatred
of things beyond her small house –
but it all happened slowly
when I was a growing lad.

I'm sure he uttered his last
misquotation long ago,
and my son lost her ashes
while I was in Budapest
in Nineteen Seventy Two –
they're both as downright dead as

they're ever likely to be
in my lifetime. What remains
is for me to hear them right:
worrying querulously
the same few mouldy old bones
as I became a poet.

In Crumpsall Library

Under the great Byzantine dome
were all the books in the wide world,
ordered and numbered on dark shelves;
and there was a long reading-room
with leathered tables at which lolled
vagrants who came to warm themselves
and ponder on the morning's news,
or study ancient magazines.
The place seemed to ask of me more
than the church where I went to praise
a God I didn't believe in,
and all those faces – like a choir –
gleaming from the stained glass windows:
Shakespeare, Homer, Cervantes, Keats,
Milton, Gray, Euripides, Burke,
looked down upon me with kind eyes –
kinder than the martyrs and saints
staring from the walls of the church –
or so I thought. I was thirteen
the library a new-found land
a mere cock's-stride from my home street.
Every day when I had done
my paper round I would ascend
the marble steps (flanked by unsweet
chasms leading to the public
conveniences – on the right
the "Ladies", on the left the "Gents")
and with quick breath and burning cheeks,
as though I were trespassing, flit
past the spectacle-flashing glance
of the lady at the counter
and on into the shadowed hush
of the stacks. I wanted to read
every book to be found there;

but I meandered in a lush
dream of knowledge among the dead
and the living, sorely afraid
that I could understand nothing.
Whether it was the serene gaze
of the noble band in mid-air,
or the hawking and loud yawning
of the vagrants in a half-doze
over their papers, I'm not sure;
but something put me at my ease,
and I was soon lost to the place
in books I couldn't understand.
A bomb blasted in the stained glass
windows one midnight. The faces
meant particular words I'd found
and read by then: no one was hurt.
Later there was a daytime raid
while I was in the library
thinking vaguely about the church
that I no longer attended.
I was skimming through a book called
Secular Modes of Religious
Experience when the sirens
started wailing. A flapping-soled
vagrant tripped, and threw me a curse
as we hurried to the basement.

Stud, Hustler, Penthouse, et al.

These acres of nakedness –
what do they mean? These calm girls
fingering their private parts
open for the dullard's gaze
in drug-stores, and the self-toils
of young boys without sweethearts?

Sometimes a rigid penis
lurks in the vicinity,
while a well-manicured hand
resolutely exposes
the viscous, pink mystery
from which we all come death-bound;

but most often these girls lie
as though the world were remote,
and aroused men a daydream
spawned by their fingers to sigh
and grunt in some foreign state
at a photograph of them.

It is done for the money,
and ignorantly, no doubt.
Meanings are not their business:
the photographer's O.K.
sends them out on a lunch-date,
or to shop for a new dress.

Nor are meanings *my* business –
I should have an erection,
to stop me thinking so much
of this abundance of flesh,
which is not meant to question
lust, loneliness, love, and such.

In New York City

Silences no traffic's roar
can muffle steal out like smells
of childhood from the backs of
eyes fixed on *Do Not Walk* lights
and meters showing cab-fares.
They are heavy; they are full
of dead people and old words:
words spoken and forgotten,
words misremembered, and words
that were never used at all.

This is a certain moment
moving, between birth and death,
towards an evening's revel.
Soon apartments are unlocked,
drinks fixed, phone-calls made to friends;
and now – safe from strangers' eyes –
in silent, scented bedrooms,
young women fresh from showers
examine the ferny vein-
patterns on their inner thighs.

Desertion, Doom, and Mistaken Identity

Before Tiskoffs came next door
a newly married couple
rented the house: the Cohens.
She was beautiful (so I
heard my mother say to my
Auntie Doris) "for her sins";
he was a big man called Phil,
who soon went off to the war.

She was related somehow
to the Goldbergs up the street,
and used to go out a lot
at night with Brenda Goldberg,
another grass-widow, fur-
coated and spindly-heeled. "What
their husbands would say I hate
to think!" seemed like an echo

I never caught the source of.
Then – among all kinds of things –
everybody heard that
Phil Cohen had deserted
from a posting in the Med.
Mrs Shindler discussed it
with my mother while broad wings
of wet washing flapped above

in the smoky breeze that blew
straight along our narrow back.
And all the other women
had ideas, too: "He's heard
of her carryings-on; word
must have reached him in Aden
or what's the name of the rock,
Gibraltar? – I ought to know."

I heard them gossiping at
yard-doors as I went about
my games and errands. But soon
they returned to rations, raids,
Tommy Handley and small kids;
as though Mrs Cohen's doom
(quickly approaching) were not
one with their virtuous spite.

Was I so perceptive when
I was eleven years old?
Thirty seven years later
and four thousand miles away
I would laugh at any guy
who asked. Or would I say: "Sure;
we were bombed; many were killed;
it made adults of children"?

Which reminds me of the Yanks
I used to see emerging
from next door – Army Air Corps
sergeants, rushing back to camp
at Burtonwood in the damp
early-morning air before
the part-blacked gas lamp went "Ping"
at the gate, and gave three blinks

and went out. "She must be mad,
man-mad!" I heard my mother
telling my Auntie Lucille.
"God help her when *he* gets back;
he'll soon stop her little tricks,
if he doesn't maim or kill
her or something or other.
She'll wish she'd not heard of bed!"

But Phil didn't return, and
she didn't change her bold ways.
Not that I cared greatly what
grown-ups did or didn't do,
as long as they left me to
the secret life of croft, street,
entry and ginnel – the maze
of the district, with its blind

alleys and sudden vistas
where bombs had opened long views;
still, when Mrs Cohen *did*
meet her doom, on a cold day
about ten months later, I
was thrilled and horrified.
Trying to make a fire blaze
in her kitchen grate she was

burned to death when her nightgown
went up in flames. The police
who came to her funeral
were on the lookout for Phil,
I heard Mrs Shindler tell
my mother. "What sort of fool
do they think he is, to chase
after the slut now she's gone?"

The Tiskoffs, Morris and Bel,
moved in after the kitchen
had been repaired. She was plain;
he was Unfit for Service,
a bald, bowlegged man with
flat feet. They used to moan
at each other all the time –
we could hear them through the wall.

An age later, when I thought
of little but my next chance
with Shirley Hoffman's bare breasts
in her mother's dark front room,
I was standing in a dream
one night with my risen lust
big in my pocket. No hints
escaped the houses of light

within – the back where I lurked
beside the air-raid shelter
was still Black-Out dark. Some twigs
tickled my face: they hung down
from the tabernacle lean-
to Mr Mantel had rigged
beside his yard-privy for
Succoth. Then, out of the dark,

two giant shapes came at me
and pushed me against the bricks
with their chests. "You are Cohen,"
one of them said. "No! Connor,"
I said. "Cohen," the other
said. "Connor," I said again.
"Cohen" – "Connor" – "Cohen" – six
or seven times the silly

antiphon was repeated.
"We are detectives," one said.
"Well, I am only fourteen,"
I said, frightened. "I live *there*
with my mam." "So you're Connor,
eh?" the other said. "Well, run
off home – you should be in bed.
Go on, now, there's a good lad!"

A Face

Catching it in shop windows
I'm always mildly surprised
by the fixed, ferocious scowl
it gives me back: as though praise
were something to be refused
on any terms, any scale.

Arranged for its owner's view
it is more amenable
to compliments and kind thoughts.
The level look seems to say:
"I acknowledge I'm a fool,
but not the worst hereabouts."

Then there's its passionate life –
which I'm sure I'll never know:
how it behaves in private
when I forget it in grief,
anger, terror, pity, joy,
or feeding an appetite.

Sometimes I awake to blind
lips puzzling its stubbled cheek,
fingers tracing its forehead;
as though it were neither owned
nor remembered in that dark,
where all social selves are shed.

But mostly it's on display
in politic, daily guise,
to make a good impression.
Perhaps you've seen it, and know
its affable, worldly ways?
I've only you to go on.

Reminiscences Remembered

for F. K.

"It must have been the summer
of '28. Fordie had
taken me to visit one
of Proust's minor Duchesses ..."

The old poet, another
tale begun, nodded his head
as though in confirmation
of a better time than this –
and I thought we and the place
no more than mist on a pane
through which he gazed easily
backwards on youth and greatness.
Now, speaking from Olympus
himself, he did not disdain
the greedy questions and sly
notetaking of those whom booze
had made unmannerly, nor
did he sneer at the breathless
student poet who said: "Wow! –
you actually *knew* Yeats?!"
Better to say he showed no
marked interest in *Tiny's
Modern Café*, and the young
faculty members who'd lured
him there to bask in the glow
of his reminiscences –
although it was ferreting
Americans who'd flattered
him from his forgotten hole
in northern England onto
Olympus and SUNY at
Buffalo.

                    "Yes, Eliot
didn't hit it off at all
with Isadora. He threw,
or tried to throw, Ezra's coat
from the window of her flat,
as a gesture of protest
at Isadora's neatness.
I should say 'her studio' –
which was bare, completely bare;
as – so it must be confessed –
was 'Dora, who greeted us
in the hall stark naked!"
                              Now
someone replenished his beer
in the reverent silence;
a Black Mountain person
asked a question about Pound's
understanding of *breath-pause*.
The old poet looked askance
at the glass he'd just put down,
and said:
                    "Cat's-piss! – which reminds
me of that cat Willie was
always fondling: Minnaloushe.
Used to pedicure its paws,
claimed it had psychic powers –
especially after it peed
all over George Moore's valise
stuffed full with reams of his prose.
I got the tale from Arthur.
– Symons: he witnessed the deed."

I didn't stay till the end,
knowing that later he would
be persuaded to comment
on the *Cantos*, and his part
in them, and then condescend

to lift his own book and read –
or utter in mannered chant –
the measured words of his art.

His private being, shrunken
and myopic, occupied
the apartment next to mine –
where, sometimes, I'd visit him.
With memory fixed upon
himself among the great dead,
the rest of his mind would strain
nobly to deal with the dim
fellow-countryman he saw
in the room. Once, speaking with
a patrician politeness,
he said:
            "I daresay that now,
the future of poetry,
of poetry in English –
if it has a future – lies
with unschooled fellows like you."

He followed this with some
words in a foreign language
unfamiliar to me:

"Which, to be more accurate
than Fitzgerald – if more lame,
I translate as:
            'Jamshýd, Mage
and Master, in the windy
ruins of your Peacock Court
an ignorant tribesman sings
as he kindles his dung-fire.'"

It was not for me to laugh
at the self-serving fictions
that give poetry its wings,

so I passed him a fresh beer,
lowering my head as if
put in my place and chastened.

He endeared himself to me
by late summer: he refused
to allow the library,
or anybody, to tape
his reminiscences.
                "No,
my boy: I won't have them *used*.
Damn these university
confidence-tricksters, in lip-
service to literature!
They want articles, footnotes,
anything in black and white
that'll help 'em get tenure.
I'll see the sods in hell-fire
before they transcribe my thoughts
and ramblings into their neat
effete books on *Belles Lettres!*"

He'd flushed such a fearsome red
that Gertrude Stein's description
of him did not seem inapt,
or even caricatured.
I saw us both reflected,
like grotesque father and son,
in the mirror that said *PABST*,
where Tiny stood embowered
among pewter mugs, bottles,
girlie posters and joke cards.
The old poet shook his head,
as though to be rid of flies.
He popped a couple of pills
into his mouth, muttered: "Turds!"
saw me beside him, and said:

"There are lies, and there are lies.
What you'll remember of me —
years from now, in some pub, say,
or perhaps in a poem,
speaking from the pure pleasure
of telling a good story —
will be warped, changed, pulled awry
into your own idiom.
You'll soon make *my* stories *your*
stories — that's how it should be.
Murrain take accuracy!
Speak with a rich man's freedom,
leave facts to the sober poor!"

The Crowd at My Door

Many people who are dead
address me within my head,

some with a vague nod and smile
as we pass at a turnstile,

some with familiar words
from beside kitchen cupboards.

Others are more troublesome:
they hover outside my home,

ambiguous, bold and sly,
waiting to importune me.

They grip my arm, and bluster,
they run fingers through lank hair,

they laugh, cajole, threaten, weep,
like actors in third-rate Rep.

They call me "Love"; "Sir"; "You swine";
"Bud"; "Holiness"; and "Bo's'n."

I can't find out what they want,
or why they choose me to haunt,

or who each one thinks I am –
for none of them knows my name.

And they keep switching titles,
as though all were death-rattles –

one as good as another:
"Dad" a ghost moans, then "Mother."

When I question them they grow
wild-eyed with wordless sorrow;

when I sweep them to one side
they clamour loudly "Coward!" ...

"You broke my heart!" ... "I sinned!" ...
"The women and children drowned!" ...

"Kiss me!" ... "Intercede!" ... "Forgive!" ...
"You do not know how to love!" ...

I can't have them arrested –
no policemen walk my head –

so I bear their harassment,
their obscure, riddling intent;

although I stay home for days,
all shades drawn against their eyes.

Domestic Poems

Proem: To the Unwary Reader

Do not study these verses
thinking to find me in them.
I hurried out to follow
old friends leaving in hearses,
and am not expected home
till they pay me what they owe.

My feelings are well hidden,
unreachable and remote.
I disowned them in childhood
and threw them on a midden:
all roads leading to the spot
have been declared closed for good.

Nor shall your like discover
what meanings I mean to share.
I speak from a dark closet,
where I fondle a lover
whose flesh is dust, and whose bare
bones sharper than my sharp wit.

1 *Bringing in the House-Plants*

A few of them are foundlings –
here's one I picked from a pot
someone had smashed on the street –
but most of them were given
with pictures and other things
unwanted, or not quite worth
space in a U-Haul. A north
wind blows: now they must live in.

I should have moved them sooner;
perhaps I wished for a frost
to come like a silent ghost,
one night while I was asleep,
and kill them off? I prefer
to believe I've been harassed,
busy, with no time to waste
on thinking of their hardship: –

(Committee meetings, the young
making new demands, women
forcing into the open
this and that and the other …
"If I've done anything wrong,
I'm sorry," I said to her.
"Oh, that's always your answer,"
she said – just like my mother.)

Anyway, these plants don't seem
to have suffered, although dead
leaves blown from the part-naked
trees lie thick around them, all
over the porch. In the dim
rooms of my house they won't thrive,
but I'll give them enough love
to ensure their survival.

If "love" is the right word for
daily fussing and fretting
over *Snake Plant, Gossip's Tongue,*
Wandering Jew and the rest
of the bastardized creatures.
I don't know why I keep them –
unless it's their obscure claim
to be my wards, and my guests.

2 *Dealing With a Stench*

When a foul stench permeates
the entire house everyone
starts to feel guilty. We glance
at one another askance –
as though civilization
were being betrayed by farts.

The stink of skunk drifting in
through open summer windows
does not question the order
of things, nor does the odour
of cast-off sweaty gym-shoes
in corners of the kitchen;

it's the abomination
with no locatable source
that trembles the edifice
of our self-esteem – like lice
in clean underwear, or worse,
obscene phone-calls to children.

So it was that my household,
waking to greet a new day
and breakfast this fine morning,
was scattered without warning
by an unknown enemy
corrupting its cleanly world.

Who or what perpetrated
the outrage nobody stayed
to enquire. As though the house
were dangerously noxious
all fled, leaving me to brood –
ashamed, and self-polluted.

Then, in a foetid corner
where I was searching, reason
reminded me of a time
four years ago, and the slime
I found in the underpan
of the refrigerator.

The forgotten pan – of course!
With held breath and wrinkled nose
I did what I had to do,
pleased to settle the issue
and avert obscure disgrace,
there at the infection's source.

3   Emptying the Fishtank

First the algaed plastic plants
are eased from their holding stones
and dumped in soapy water,
then the decorative shells.

   Lifting the sunken vessels
is trickier: they splatter
the counter with blobs like blains
on gangrenous flesh – their joints
oozing a vile sediment
as I swing them to the sink.

   Next the goldfish must be caught
(where they blunder frantically
through an element, thickly
clouded with I-don't-know-what
stirred-up matter) and dropped, *plonk*,
plonk, *plonk* into a new haunt –
the old zinc bucket waiting
on the floor to receive them.

   The entire operation
takes about ninety minutes,
and depresses my spirits
with its insistence upon
the universe as a slum
that can't be kept clean for long;
nevertheless I always
recover my good humour
before it's done – perhaps by
seeing myself from the point
of view of a fish, or (faint
but swelling) by hearing high
hosts of angels in a choir
Magnifying Me with Praise.

4 Taking a Bath

When I was born I arrived
trailing clouds of misery,
whose slow evaporation
has left me at last naked,
and ready to be beloved
by the obscure deity
who watches such things happen,
though they spring from his own head.

As a child, youth, and young man,
I hated getting undressed:
the bathtub was a low place
where I averted my eyes
from the corporal human
encumbrance, that shat and pissed
and did other things much worse,
which I could hardly surmise.

With age the misery's gone.
I sit here pleased and amused
by the sharp, female fragrance
that still clings to my upper
body, and was sharpest on
the primary organ used –
now lolling like a tired prince
half-asleep in warm water.

I've got two nakednesses mixed,
but no matter: my bathtub-
speculations at fifty
dream away demarcations
till nothing's discrete or fixed –
the flesh and spirit hobnob,
and women and God both say:
"Quiet – that room's the children's!"

5   *Defrosting the Freezer*

Dammit! What fun's a fine house
when nobody shares the work
or contributes to payment
of the bills?
                  "Find a new spouse,"
a voice suggests, "and earmark
some money – that'll be spent
otherwise on nightly beer –
to hire a cleaning-lady
for one afternoon a week.
No use playing the martyr:
we've seen that act already;
you're simply egocentric –
you want to do everything
yourself, to be an Atlas
with the world on your shoulders."

"Oh, shut up!" I think (wasting
no breath on the emptiness
as I get on with my chores),
and the voice succumbs to loud
interior moans, grumbles,
and complaints against my lot.

Now *this* job's a real sod!
It enrages me and dulls
my wits at the same time. But
who'll do it if I don't?
Worse – it can't even be rushed!
The one time I tried to spear-
off the rime with a knife point
I punctured the lining, gashed
my hand, and got a repair-
bill and two stitches to show

for my trouble.
               "Come off it!"
the voice says. "That's a bald lie."

"I'm not arguing with you,"
I mutter, nursing my
fate of literate drudgery.

6 Not Cleaning the Windows

Which poet was it that thought
poems should be transparent –
much like panes of window-glass
which don't attract attention
to themselves unless some flaw
makes the prospect they present
seem blurred, bent, or otherwise
distorted and part-undone?

I don't know. But he left out –
I dare say circumspectly –
the coating of dirt and dust
that builds on every window
to obscure and cast in doubt
the point of the simile,
because it may be erased
in favour of a clearer view.

Still, I carry a bucket,
a squeegee and sponge-mop,
and I'm high up a ladder
with a lot of work to do –
this is no time to speculate
on poetry, I may drop
something, or come a cropper
on the concrete path below.

What's more, I must insist on
windows remaining windows
if I'm to finish my task
of washing and polishing
back, sides, front, upstairs, and down,
every last pane in the house
before the onset of dusk,
or the beginning of spring.

I've postponed it for so long
(seven years, to be exact –
since I first came to live here!)
and still I procrastinate,
babbling on with double-tongue
as though I were in the act,
while I bang the typewriter
and try to keep my thoughts straight.

7 Making a Din with the Vacuum-Cleaner

Telemann could never have
imagined what would happen
to his music. All those years
of mute burial, and then
a bursting up from the grave
to appreciative cheers!

Still, he was a wise old bird,
who tried to please the patron,
and succeeded. No doubt that
was enough. Wouldn't unborn
patrons have been an absurd
audience for him to court?

Good artists don't make bequests
to the future. Shakespeare went
with a shrug of foul papers:
he knew nothing could prevent
his voices shrinking to ghosts
who'd squeak bleakly in Hades –

or lexicographers' minds,
to abandon metaphor.
And long before the final
snuffing-out (whether by war,
or live wastes breaking their bonds
in some deep ocean channel)

householders reading *Hamlet*
to Telemann's music, will
obliterate both to groom
living-room, kitchen and hall,
so that the place will look neat
when next week's visitors come.

8 *Listening to the Heating System*

More ominous than a ghost
in the cellarage, the sound
of the furnace turning on
interrupts my play of thought –
already under attack
from pains in the leg and back.
How to work a poem out,
with that infernal machine
chunnering of OPEC and
what this winter's warmth will cost!

It's an old story, all right:
family, and politics,
and ills the flesh is heir to
bring many a noble mind
to its knees (the metaphor
is mixed: – my knee-joints are sore).
Shall I renounce my first bond,
and send the children away?
rent a smaller house? – buy stocks
in Oil, and go corporate?

Of course not; I'll soldier on
paying monthly heating bills,
and grumbling about the size
of this wide, three-storied house,
while I try to write good verse,
and my arthritis gets worse.
No lunges at the arras –
I lack the wild miseries
that construct their own death cells;
mine is an open prison.

Someone has padded talcum-
powder all over the house;
or are these a ghost's footprints?
Aimless peregrination
it seems to me, as I track
the spoor down the back stairway
from the bathroom (where it starts)
to the kitchen, and across
the living-room carpet
into the hall. Following
the milky, translucent marks
up the front stairs, I find them
entering all the bedrooms: –
what's going on here? I think;
is there some promiscuous
spirit abroad in my house –
are my next-door neighbours
correct in their suspicions?
I'm sure they'd say:"Without doubt!"
finding thickly spread powder
in front of the toilet bowl –
where one of my teen-age sons
dusted his bathed and dried flesh
with half a canister-full
of talc, – and realizing
that fourteen feet have spread it:
broadcasting private journeys
as though the many were one.

A Small Annoyance

The Italian's pigeons
sit on the telephone wire
outside my bedroom window:
I am wakened by the row
from their ragged, cooing choir
long before the day begins.

All summer the fat old man
potters about his green yard
among tomatoes and vines;
to complain of his pigeons
would brand me as ill-tempered –
they are his senile passion.

So I curse them in private,
and wave to him as I weed
my struggling vegetables.
Three houses away, he smiles,
and strokes a held pigeon's head
before urging it skyward.

On the Violent Death of a Dog

The dog who hanged himself from
our back porch had had enough
of the world and of his home.
The roses in feeble leaf
at the end of the garden
seemed to offer him reproof
for not being under them,
and the sad tomato plants
said, "If only you lay dumb
among the hidden events
deep beneath our roots, what large
and succulent fruit we'd flaunt
next summer!" The poor dog's urge
to end it all and be done
teetered on the very edge
of an ultimate action,
as Great Sustaining Nature
wooed and beckoned to her son.
He was the inheritor
of savage melancholy
from his nondescript father,
and a tendency to flee
the world of men from his dam
(a bitch without pedigree):
yet, when it seemed that the sum
of his life was about to
be totalled, his little frame
trembled its entire length through
with love late-recognized in
admonishment, kick and blow,
the cruelty of children,
grisly scraps tossed at his feet,
and the tyranny of chain,
now asserting its limit –
though tangled around him twice.

My neighbour who witnessed it
(mystical female sympathies
give her understanding of
animals) told me all this.
She had thought, she said, the brave
animal's suicidal
torments resolved. "Live and Love!"
was the message of the tail
she observed to be wagging
as though of its own sweet will;
and so, when the kettle sang
out suddenly in her house,
without a qualm or a pang
of foreboding she had raced
in to placate it. But, O!,
at that moment Thanatos
decided to claim his due,
and by dark befuddlements
push settled purpose awry.
With never a backward glance,
and only a joyful "Woof"
(my neighbour has told me since)
the dog hurled himself from off
the porch, to die in mid-air
when the chain snapped neck and life.
What a fiction! She should pour
her imaginings into
poetry, where some are sure
such stuff belongs. As for me:
I released the stiff remains
and put them to make plants grow.

   The Epitaph

Here lies BUZZ, his blood and bones
useful at last. That is that.
Possessing very few brains,
he hanged, jumping for a cat.

My Mother Singing

My mother sang: "There's a long,
long trail a-winding into
the land of my dreams," and steam
came drifting up with the song
from the cellar-boiler she
stood over, filling rooms
and corridors with odours
of wet washing. Her Monday
chore took hours and hours: sometimes
she was still at it downstairs
when I arrived home for tea –
water sloshing and dull rhymes
thumping. "Where the nightingale
is singing and the bright moon
beams." The songs were always from
the trenches of Passchendaele
and the Somme, where the young men
she might have married became
corpses she couldn't mourn. Now,
over twenty years later,
she had been long abandoned
by the stunned survivor who
gave her two children, and there
was another war to end
war, and she took in washing,
and no young man dreamed of her
as he dozed in a dugout;
but she was fit and strong,
and who could say what was fair
or what life was all about?
I am putting thoughts into
the head that sings in my head –

a man the age she was then.
In truth I will never know
why she sang, and she is dead,
like all her "lovely young men".

The Voices

It is not a litany;
most of the time there is no
response, or there is a sigh
or a mumble or a slow
sobbing like someone alone
with a grief beyond sorrow
in the next room.

              Then the phone
rings, and it is the living
with demand, invitation,
advice, or full listening
silence – nothing like the deep
self-absorption of the long-
dead.
       Sometimes when I'm asleep
they will speak in the voices
of distant trains, and the drip
of late raindrops from roses,
and the sigh of wind-stirred trees
at the back of the houses;
but these are merely echoes
telling me of things I know:

"In winter the ground will freeze."

"I studied all day today."

"The frying pan is greasy."

"High is high and low is low."

Aubade

"Mr Nobody," I thought,
when the bedroom door rattled
scattering my pleasant dream
of childhood. The dawn light boomed
and soughed as the wind battled
trees and houses in the street;
already the hammers were
declaring their flat dogmas
in Wilcox and Crittenden's
Marine Hardware factory;
already the whining roar
of the garbage truck, zealous
in its crushings and grindings,
was waking sleepers nearby.
"Mr Nobody," I thought,
wrapping my dream around me
(or was it the bedcovers)
and I was far from lovers:
their bold comings, their sulky
goings – their sly-passionate,
guarded goings at first light
or whenever. I was back
in *A Child's Garden of Verses*,
and in the child reading it
a long time ago. I thought
later (when I was awake
enough to acknowledge her
fading imprint on the sheet,
her scent on the pillowcase)
that I did not know her name,
or what she had been doing
in my room. Such are the strong
resistances I bring home
from all my acts of darkness.

Lost Love

I was thinking of lost love,
or trying to think, across
the bad-mouthing of my heart
(which would not stop its insults),
and a pop-song about love
drivelling from somewhere close
to the chair in which I sat
waiting for a girl whose faults
I was not yet aware of.
   It was a busy lunch-hour
in the Delicatessen;
but I was trying to think
of a time and place and love
vanished into the thin air
of what cannot come again,
so my mind kept going blank.
   The best that I could manage
were a few vivid day-dreams:

making love through her wild tears
just after her mother's death
("She should have been on the stage,"
my heart said); the blue-veined domes
of her nursing breasts; the stairs
with the baby's crib beneath;
her anger when she found out
my worst infidelity
("You were always a lecher,"
my heart said); the way she smiled
one night in kitchen firelight,
after I left my study
and came to confer with her
on making another child.

("*This* is thinking of lost love?"
my heart said – or the spirit
of the Delicatessen),
and a man with a tray
gave me an impatient shove
as he sidled to a seat.
"Oh honey, do it again!"
sang the pop-group from L.A.,
then I saw my latest girl
shaking the snow from her hat
near the door. From a distance
she looked like Zenobia,
or some undismayable
Goddess; but she was too late
to catch me as I was once –
not that she would have liked me.

Middle Age

Call it a settled habit
after twenty years or more –
this sitting in the evening
with a blank page before me,
waiting for words that might
tell me what I mean. I fare
badly most nights: phones ring,
doors slam, the lodger's hi-fi
thumps its bass down through two floors,
my daughter comes for a kiss
before bed, my sons to get
the keys to the second car;
but still I persist. For hours
I sit here in bored distress
listening to a debate
taking place in the mind's ear –
a debate about nothing
and everything, the secret
subject of which is rarely
identifiable in
the babel of stammering
voices. Sometimes I forget
my responsibility,
and don't listen. Then a stain
on the edge of the blotter
takes me back to the kitchen
of my childhood, or a smell
curls from nowhere, and again
I'm well-married to her
whose body, cool and open,
moves beneath mine as I feel-
out the form of a poem.

6

from *Spirits of the Place*
(1986)

Child and Man

Here is a snapshot of me –
twine-toed, doubtful, two years old –
throwing a ball at a gate.
Any infant, it could be:
I can't think of that large-skulled
creature as my intimate.

And yet I must, I suppose:
an unbroken thread of thoughts,
feelings, dreams and what-have-you,
leads from big head and twine-toes
to the professor who sits
here with new glasses askew.

I study him in the black
window across my workdesk;
he peers at me from the night,
as though to say: "Now this tack
brings no gain, and puts at risk
the poem you wish to write."

Well, I don't know about that;
but the little chap's no chance
against my shadowy twin,
who specializes in flat
denials, and good hard sense,
when dealing with reckless kin.

Best draw the curtains – shut out
his face, and middle-aged cant.
He likes aborting new things,
while I play on through my doubt,
as dead-set as this infant
on what the next second brings.

In John B's Café

Wendell fist-fights the juke-box,
swearing he's lost a quarter.
"Fucking bitch juke-box!" he shouts.

Vinnie says, "Cool it will ya!"
He moves from behind the bar,
shifts the juke-box sedately:
soon it bellows forth *That's Life*.

Wendell grins, he sways, he mimes
to the voice of Sinatra –
mouth working, head back, arms wide-
pumping the beer-weary air.

Vinnie leans across the bar,
smoking, watching the display.
"You won't see *him* tomorrow"
he tells me. "Soon as the cops
realize he's loose again
they'll move him on – the goddam
lunatic! – straight out of town."

That's Life comes to an end
with Wendell stretched, crucified,
eyes screwed tight in ecstasy.

"Ah, the guy's crazy, but shit,
he never done me no harm,"
Vinnie says; "Let the guy sing!
Let the guy enjoy himself."

At the Entrance to Wadsworth State Park

Beyond bright bodywork, trees
offer their invitation
to enter another world –
to make good use of Sundays.
Supermarkets are open,
(the old "blue laws" were repealed
a month before Christmas) but
even the secular soul
needs some respite from commerce –
or so I tell myself at
the sight of a clearing full
of cars, wagons and trailers.

Usually my weekend
walk is a solitary,
brooding business: all winter
the forest has been snowbound
or deep in mud – I don't see
ten walkers from November
to April ahead of me
in the trees.
        The old poet
of New England himself might
well have found his dark fancy
moved into writing of it:
here is a tumbled wall that
once divided properties;
there is the grown-over ghost
of the road between hamlets
more ghostly still; here fruit trees
of an abandoned orchard;
there (if you search) broken pots
from a long-gone farm kitchen.

But today is different:
it looks as if half the town
is inside the forest, bent
on enjoying union
with Nature. Perhaps I should
come back tomorrow, I think –
irresolutely jiggling
the shift-stick of my battered
Toyota.
        Nearby a drunk
is aiming a mumbled song
at the forest as he weaves
between close-parked vehicles,
and – waddling out from the trees –
a fat family arrives
back on known ground, with squabbles
about Wendy's and Hardee's.

In Retirement

The old man ambles sag-kneed,
busy about his back yard.
From spring's first warmth to late fall
he goes from job to job, staid
and purposeful – working hard,
but without semblance of toil.

I savour him in my thought:
he rests within his motions
as a good labourer will,
when he has chosen his lot.
Dreams of order and patience
inform such slowness, such skill.

He moves firmly, like a sleep-
walker, between growing green
and sawn firewood roughly stacked.
Undistractably in step
with some internal vision
of set tasks not to be shirked.

I watch him straighten the stack
from my yard two lawns away:
enjoying his absorption,
which will hold till nearly-dark.
Finished, he stakes a bean-row,
then stretches to trim a vine.

The scene's clearly in focus
as I rest within the lines
forming beneath my pencil,
and sleepwalk towards my purpose –
absorbed in working visions
of grace, growth and things done well.

Woolworth's: Main Street on Saturday

The obscurely hoping poor
wander, zombie-listless, brains
junk-deadened, from aisle to aisle.

Gnarled hands turn then abandon
a card of identical
mock mother-of-pearl buttons:
great-grandchildren without names.

From a jungle of houseplants
(On Special Springtime Offer)
African darkness stares
sleeping with eyes open –
pursuers long forgotten,
or now being dreamed to death.

Bunioned feet inveigle
plastic-soled slippers, easing
their birthright-discomfort in.

A life that cannot recall
how it should fit together
buys a tube of Krazy Glue
guaranteed to hold two tons.

At the luncheonette counter,
faces, pimply-vacuous,
open and close on burgers –
not looking at one another,
like survivors of a blast.

Outside, under a wide sky
festive with vaporous trails
from peace-protecting warplanes,
the beautiful cars go by,
their occupants thinking of
sport, sex, business, art, bombs, love.

My Pipes

Many, in the way of things,
have been broken or lost – where
and how I can't remember;
yet they were all my darlings:
each one in its time a rare
companion and comforter.

For their service – forgotten.
Every individual
shape, balance, texture, solace,
merged in a master-pattern:
the Platonic Ideal
of what I stick in my face.

The survivors – a poor lot
lolling about in the rack
without useful employment –
I can differentiate
too well: blocked, sour, hot to smoke,
light, loose-jointed, leaky, bent.

But the one I'm puffing now –
a peerless pipe, a fine friend –
is bound for oblivion.
Dropped, or snapped, or lost somehow
from my fondest care, its end
is a foregone conclusion.

The Act

The necessary prelude
is a beautiful woman
undressing in a still room,
intrigued and slightly afraid: –
she is expecting someone.

Her latest lover, no doubt –
why else stare long in the glass,
tease hair, smooth lips, accent eyes?
Holding a gem to her throat
she admires her nakedness.

This is a scene from a play,
and she is a great actress
who cannot make a wrong move.
Let her stumble, stammer, sigh:
all is controlled; nothing loose.

Small wonder things go awry
when I enter – my heart hers,
and in my mouth! O true, true,
my trembling smile, my stiff bow,
my unresourceful gestures!

Aphrodite

She lolls on me drunkenly,
moaning about her troubles
in blurred lies, as usual, –
that still-magnificent face
turning mascara smudges,
lipstick smears and a black eye
into grotesque beauty marks.
"I'm going to end it all,"
she snivels into my tear-
wet lapel.
          I put my arm
around her beefy shoulders
and lean against the counter,
taking the booze-heavy load
as best I may – other arm
pinned by her once shapely breasts.

All I might say I have said
to her unlistening ears
on earlier such evenings.
My patient kindness bores me
with its patent uselessness,
yet I repeat and repeat
soothing words, as to a child,
while trying to manoeuvre
her carcass onto a chair.

With luck she'll drink some coffee,
smoke a cigarette or two,
and head for another bar
or perhaps she wants to fuck –
in which case my luck's run out,

and I'll find myself serving
sorrows beyond remedy,
itches beyond assuagement
in a region where kindness
vomits out its own sweet name.

Routes to the Liquor Store

In terms roughly understood,
misunderstood, and beyond
my comprehension, the world
continuously imagines
new versions of itself in
my head. I've been puzzled
by the drifts of our loose bond
ever since early childhood.

Now, settled at fifty-two,
I'm impatient with such thoughts,
such ways to get through a verse,
unless they lead me somewhere.
Like routes to the liquor store
on which I dawdle, and pause
brooding on new-made lines taut
as high summer's timeless blue,

or on people seen at ease
through open doors on warm nights
when summer is nearly done:
survivors of one more day,
who sprawl in chairs, or argue
with unseen others, or scan
magazines, or switch off lights
to stare out at the dark trees.

Interrupted Gardening

Some trick of decrepit flesh
gives her eyes a death-wise look:
a glance from beyond the grave.

What such death-wisdom might be
I've no idea, of course;
in garden terms, evening terms –
the terms by which I'm tending
my tomatoes (binding here,
clipping there, nimble-fingered
and keen-eyed to root out weeds
and tiny shoots of crabgrass) –
she leans: crooked, stroke-stricken,
on her walking-companion
at the end of my driveway.
A tedious old lady,
who's always lived on this street.

Unwilling to pass me by,
it seems, she croaks something down
the thirty yards between us –
wobbling words, gusted away
by the ghost of a slight breeze.
I wave and smile (still crouching),
catching not one syllable.
She croaks again – and again
I can't hear what she's saying,
though I nod understanding,
and shout: "Glad to see you out!"

Now I think her silent stare
is empty of all judgement –
like a newly born infant's.

I wish they'd go on their way,
she and her companion.

Which they do – unseen by me –
while I'm rising and twirling,
dodging and jumping about
to avoid a bumblebee's
interest in my bare chest.
When I return to the plants
the driveway is deserted.

Even though my knee-joints hurt
I like crouching near these leaves:
evening brings out their fragrance,
and I'm not bothered too much
by the clusters of aphids
I find under some of them.
The many yellow flowers
augur a heavy harvest,
the plants are healthy and tall,
outgrowing my wooden stakes.

There'll be great, globous beauties
by the laundry-basketful
before fall's gone – I can taste
that ripe fruit-flesh already!

Last Things

It's a trivial enough
ceremony – turning off
all the houselights before bed;
every night for years I made
little of it. Othello
must have come to my mind
now and then, and Grey (wasn't it?)
with his "Lights are going out
all over Europe"; but not
to distress or disturb thought,
as I journeyed slowly from
lamp to lamp and room to room,
beneath children fast asleep
in my careful stewardship.

       ★   ★   ★

That account's idealized:
sometimes I came home well-soused
when my favourite bar closed
at one a.m. – sharp with lust
for the girl I'd brought with me …
Now I see what Othello
and Grey are doing up there –
images of love and war!
Reminders of revenge-fits,
of passion's poisonous fruits.
Or, to be more specific,
the woman who tried to choke
the life from me as I slept;
and the sullen girl who stripped
cursing, then, out of malice,
fused every light in the house;

and those two who tumbled down
disputing dominion,
to slap and scratch and pull hair
all over the kitchen floor.

　　　★　★　★

That account's misleading, too;
I plough a lonely furrow,
most often taking to bed
words with which I'm enamoured –
words like "Othello" and "Grey"
that titillate and annoy.
And so it has been for years,
apart from a few affairs
when the children were asleep,
and I made a brief escape
from fatherhood.
　　　　　　　Trivial
ceremonies: the simple,
repetitive acts by which
we ennoble what we botch –
or hope to ennoble, – these
have been the anonymous
masters of my past decade.
After so long I abide
by them still, feeling a fool
as often as not, but ill-
able to stop myself. Soon
I'll make the journey again
that pronounces day ended
(though these nights I'm off to bed
long before my sons return,
and I must leave one light on
in case they've been partying,
and come home blindly stumbling);
maybe Othello, or Grey,

or both will accompany
my darkening pilgrimage
in diminishing wattage;
maybe my age-heavy face,
nodding at the bathroom glass,
will suffice to augur mind
dead and lightless at its end.

Genesis of the Poet

Fog gusted outside our house,
and crept in through every crack.
Frank Mounsor, fresh from the pub,
was pushing his lodger's luck.

The streetlamp's shrouded gaslight
hardly reached to our front door;
he dropped his key, then fell down,
misquoting lines from *King Lear*.

Once in the hallway he sang
"Rock of ages left for me ...";
a coat-rack moved to trip him,
he kicked it out of the way.

Stumbling through the middle room
he garbled an ode by Scott,
and reached the kitchen at last,
where my mother and I sat.

I looked up from my homework;
my mother said: "Well, he's here!"
The coal fire burned bright and warm
in the kitchen's foggy air.

Frank Mounsor threw his cap off,
it hit the wall with a thud.
He smiled vaguely, stretched, yawned, belched;
"The rest is silent," he said.

But how could he be silent,
primed to eloquence by ale –
he, who loved the sound of verse
as he loved a bellyful?

Posturing unsteadily,
he waved an imagined sword,
and started to bellow forth
"The Charge of the Light Brigade".

My mother took no notice;
I giggled and went to bed,
where I fell into sweet dreams
through slewed rhythm and slurred word.

Irk

People said if you fell in
you'd be poisoned before drowned.

Black, stinking, garbage-littered,
it burbled belyingly
through Bowker Bank, and sneaked
out of my direct knowledge
under scum-bearded barbed wire
siding Union Carbide.

Near Victoria Station,
from the top deck of a bus
curving into the city,
there it was again – far down
on waste ground beneath Crown Bridge –
spilling filth into more filth
where its foul mouth fed Irewell.

But that wasn't my river,
whose dark, secret God
watched over holiday games
from the rhododendron-glooms
that uttered it to the vale
at the Titan Dye Works end.

My river ran no farther
than the length of Bowker Bank,
rank and taken for granted,
like a sourceless schoolroom fart –
and as much part of childhood.

Unconscious of business-greed,
industrial pollution,
Acts, facts and figures of trade,
my river runs on through dreams
of smoke-heavy afternoons
and grubby, cloud-streaked sunsets.
The God watching, never seen;
the boy running in the stench,
or prone above, staring down
through shrunken, chinked, bridge-boarding
at that eye-filling turmoil,
that bottom-blind fishless flow –

marvellous, deadly water!

My Mother, with Maiden Ladies

When the First World War began
my mother was twenty-one.
Dreaming of marriage, no doubt,
and the love that went with it.
By the time the war ended
everything had gone bad.
Slouching back, blank-eyed, hot-groined,
came the wounded, mad and stunned,
babbling of dead men, or mute
as the corpse of a best mate.

Ten years later she married
one of the walking wounded,
whose heart was a no-man's-land,
whose thoughts rats gnawing a hand.
He gave her two kids – and then
abandoned the position.

Perhaps I was nothing more
than a souvenir of war:
some long-withheld remembrance
exchanged in the sexual dance.

Miss Butcher, Miss Briggs, Miss Mew,
Miss Henderson, Miss O'Shea,
found no one to take the place
of the man who blew a kiss
from a start-jolting troop-train:
Harry, Bert, Alf, Arthur, John.

Less lucky than my mother –
who at least found a father
for her imagined children –

they boarded, or lived alone,
nearby the house I grew in:
patient; waiting for a sign.

Talk often turned to the dead
in those dismal days I played
happily through. And voices
death-spoke from moving glasses
and the unmoving, tranced mouths
of mediums – lies or truths
to dignify hopelessness.

My mother returned breathless
one night, Miss O'Shea bright-eyed
and serious by her side –
both were full of the séance.
A message had come, through Hans,
the grumpy Danish *Control*:
"Tell Doll I am alive still –
everlastingly alive
in the Land of Divine Love,
where flowers bloom everywhere
and there is no pain – Arthur."

They chattered across my head
while I planned an action: lead
soldiers with bayonets fixed –
row upon row, newly unboxed.

A Walk Between Air Raids

"Look yonder, son, just above
t'Milky Way. That's Orion,
that is, with Rigel at t'top.
Bellatrix and Betelgeuse
are them two other bright stars."

This was my Uncle Arthur's
first sign that he had a use
for matters beyond the scope
of political action.
As far as I knew he gave
his waking attention to
nothing besides the "bloody
government", capitalist
exploitation of the poor,
and the certain revolution
when hordes of young servicemen
returned home after the war
to find the workers oppressed,
still, by men with big money –
the rulers, the evil few.

Above us clear, cloudless sky,
with no bombers and no moon;
he was accompanying
me home from his house, doubtless
to gain respite from his wife's
unending gossip – all tiffs
between women.

                    "Perseus
is *there*, left look – along
my arm; d'ye see it now, son?
And yon's Cassiopeia."

He was a skilled man: a brick-
layer, plasterer, plumber,
and master of many trades,
who couldn't keep a job long
before he roused the rabble
and got sacked for the trouble
he made on the site. He'd bring
home his toolbag and his "cards",
and sit hunched over the fire
reviling the spineless Clerk
of Works, that bosses' lackey,
and his fellow working men,
the stupid, easily duped
masses. That's how I picture
him most often: – unemployed,
and at home. Either inside,
impotent among the lore
of women; or lofty-hoped
on his allotment where, soon,
he expected to break free
from the tyranny of price-
rigging in greengrocery.

"Further left's Andromeda,
with Pegasus above. Now,
come down under t'Milky Way –
eeh, this is a grand night sky! –
see, son, where I'm pointing to,
that's the Pole Star, or North Star."

He had never talked to me
of stars. It was a surprise
to see him peering upward,
and to hear the mild awe in
his voice as the splendid names
came from between the blackened
broken teeth he cleaned with Vim.

But, stumbling beside him,
trying to watch my feet and
star-gaze, too, I made poems
that were neither of live men,
nor the stars, nor the bomb-scarred
city looming jaggedly
around our footsteps' echoes.

"D'ye see Ursa Minor there –
The Little Bear? That was t'last
thing I saw before I went
down on t'Somme. The Monument
at Salford's got me in t'list
of 'Missing In Action'; – bare-
faced wishful thinking by those
who'd like to be rid of me."

Cricket at Rawtenstall

The schoolteacher from Hapton
square-cuts for four. The crowd claps.
Someone says, "Well, here comes the rain."
I feel a few oily drops,
and clouds piled over Cribden
move in behind the slips.

Surrounding moors, blanched by sun,
look rock-naked. Blue shadow
clings to scarp, outcrop and coomb,
and stretches long from the few
farm-houses. Late afternoon
with a half-hour yet to Tea –

and the Indian pro's out!
He walks back eyeing the clouds.
The man next to me says, "Wot
a stroke! – and we've nobbut duds
left to bat. We'll be well-beat,
unless t'rain comes down in floods!"

It doesn't. A few more drops,
that's all – but the sun's gone in,
and Cribden top's under drapes
of furry, slanting cloud-rain.
The moors are louring slopes:
humpbacks that never knew the sun.

Number nine's at the wicket.
He takes elaborate guard –
to appeal against the light!
Visiting supporters gird
and shout as the umpires chat,
casting shrewd eyes heavenward.

Then play goes on. Edges, fours,
tangles of legs, a few byes,
missed runs and ironic cheers
usher in Tea. Itching boys
fall and fight. I watch the moors
Atlasing the leaden skies.

Coming my way, Jack Enstone
ambles round the boundary –
the old, Youth Hostel Christian.
Puzzled by apostasy,
he is teased and pleased by mine,
so I point my pipe, and say,

"Eh, let's have a prayer or two –
we need rain!" He shakes his head,
flapping white, wire hair, looks coy,
and says, "Now don't talk daft, lad!"
Towards Stacksteads two fields glow
where black clouds let through a rod

of revelatory light
that disappears as it came.
I leave with Jack, past the sight-
screen, to banter the way home,
and down pours all the world's wet
from sky's lightning-ripped bedlam.

A Lesson

Whatever the lesson was,
she found herself with class-time
remaining, and thirty kids
to be kept (at least) amused.
The warm, varnished-pine school-room
striped with chalk-moted sunrays,
was restless with turning heads
as text-books and minds were closed.

She was a youngish woman,
bright-eyed, and often smiling
in that depressed, war-time place;
I was a thirteen-year-old,
as useless as tangled string,
for all my "promise" and "brain".
Her favourite, nonetheless: –
she looked my way when she smiled.

She began to talk about
punishment: the leather strap –
every teacher's last recourse –
still used throughout the high school,
what did *we* think? Hands shot up
cleaving the sunrays, where motes
swirled whitely. She held the class
close in her kind, clever rule.

A much-strapped lout said his dad
thought it scandalous; his pal
swore it made you sore all day; –
everyone clamoured to speak.
I sat and watched the motes swirl,
and fade – as the sunrays did,
leaving the hullabaloo
and the wall-clock's jerky tick.

The teacher looked round the room.
"Is there anyone," she said
through my chalk-dusty daydream,
"who's never had the strap?" No
hands were raised, then my hand slid
upwards. Her smile was the same
as ever, clever and warm;
she raised one kindly eyebrow.

"So you've *never* had the strap?"
she asked incredulously;
"In all your schooldays – *never*?" –
I nodded. The sun came out,
striping the air again. "My
goodness!" she said. "Well, just step
to the front, Mr Connor" –
she liked me, I had no doubt.

"Now, hold your hand out," she said.
Hardly free of my day-dream,
I felt the strap's stinging slam
across my stretched-out fingers.
Motes swirled. The bell rang "Hometime".
I stood there with my lesson –
whatever the lesson was.

Old Soldier

Mr Orme, straightening tweeds
fragrant with shag tobacco,
addressed us in muffled words –
his false teeth gripped tight as glue
on the sheered stem of the pipe
that poked from the ragged straw
thatch hiding his upper lip:
"Juldee! you young lads, Juldee!"
    We wouldn't stay in a group:
the girls tossed indignant heads,
and dawdled more; the boys shook
one another, chased down goads,
back-kicked, tweaked ears, stopped to gawk
at rich men's shining new cars
all the way to Broughton Park.
    He shuffled ahead, a curse
against rheumatism, kids
and old age spluttering the fires
of his pipe: what were the odds
of a sergeant ending up
with the worst of awkward squads,
when he'd lost command, and grip –
his keen eye, his booming voice?
    At the park gates, with one swoop
we reached and passed him, to loose
ourselves in woods and hillocks,
and in the lake's stinking ooze.
Did I look back through squawks,
swinging braids, leaps and bright eyes,
to see his stern face relax?
Mission accomplished, at ease,
he leaned on his blackthorn stick –
no longer in charge of us.

Thus does the mind, looking back,
make counter-realities.
His name was Midgeley. He'd walk
a gang of us – on fine days –
across the dangerous road,
through the district of posh Jews,
and into Clowes Park – where he'd
sit by the scummed lake for hours
while we squabbled, fought and played.
To allay our mothers' fears,
I suppose – we were all small,
none much older than nine years.
"Your rat's a clean animal,"
he said to me once, his eyes
more watery than the dull,
soot-surfaced, rat-swum shallows
he peered across. "Good eating,
when you've gone hungry for days.
'Course, we was damn' near starving
when we shot 'em for meat stews
at the siege of Mafeking."

Walking Back to the Village: Saturday Afternoon

The Old road dipped suddenly
and swung sideways through green shade,
as though tired of open miles
on a windy ridge. The sky
and its shifting cavalcade
went behind lofty leaf-tiles.

The vicar's rickety bike
leaned at his porch. Bernard Cross
was clearing weeds from a ditch
with a scythe that flashed toy-like.
Woodpigeons coo-cooed of loss;
the air stood fragrant and rich.

The Old road met the New road
where the garden of The Swan
spilled petals on a stone yard,
and ahead the newly-mowed
village green framed Amy's son –
our last batsman – taking guard.

The House

I remember silences:
the silence of the bedroom
in which someone had gone mad;

the silence of corridors
where nobody went or came
and nothing was ever said;

I remember the silence
of the backyard at noonday
with the cat curled on a stone;

the silence of mezzotints
leapt at or lapped by shadow
when the evening firelight shone;

most of all I remember
the silence of secrecy:
of not knowing what was wrong.

This silence was my mother,
clenched on an ancient sorrow,
her harsh threnody unsung.

From India

Taking the God for a Walk

I passed them on the low road
to Bubaneshwar: four men
carrying a palanquin
in which reclined a small god.

I was in a hurry, they –
keeping the god's time, I thought –
dawdled with the deity,
smoking and dragging their feet.

A minute later I glanced back
from my bouncing, Council car:
now they were sprawled at leisure
beside an overturned truck.

The small god was resting, too:
his palanquin stood apart
beyond the truck's blue shadow,
as if holding lonely court.

Why I was hurrying so
I can't remember at all;
but I remember well
that diminishing tableau,

and raucous crowds in the town
a mile or so down the road –
awaiting with devotion
the coming of the small god.

On the Dadar Express

Headmaster with jaundiced face,
gammy-legged from old war wounds,
how we boys smirked behind hands
when you recited to us!

Never in our classroom long –
always filling some time-gap –
you'd croak, before the bell rang,
"Yes, I remember Adlestrop …"

The poem brings you to mind,
as this place brings the poem:
platform, nameboard, idling steam-
engine, a landscape of sand

somewhere in Tamil Nadu
on the day I'm fifty-three.
I wonder at both of you
for coming so far with me!

Dinner Party, Baroda

"I am old and I am blind:
despised and dying!"
                           The words
resound on the hot night air
without disturbing the moths
around the verandah lamps,
or the large, flowering plants
in their brass bowls, or the guests
sipping bootleg Madras Scotch.

   "Is nonsense," our hostess says,
shifting her short, fat body
so that her wicker chair squeaks.
"We are having a nice drink,
just as we usually do
after dinner. Und your drink
now it is beside your hand –
do not spill it."
                           Her husband
sits with bowed head, his eyes closed
behind thick, useless lenses;
silenced forever, it seems.

   "Ach, he will go to bed soon,"
she says.
                           Her guests resume talk
of prohibition:
                           "My word,
the bloody politicians! –
Don't we know they drink like fish
while pretending to be good
followers of Gandhiji!"

   Dr Das giggles about
'The Princess':
                           "Foolish Bubbles,
for letting that young woman
into the palace! Ahmed

had more vigour than she knew –
to be a father again
at seventy! She should blame
herself, oh yes, not the girl."

Something reminds our hostess
of her youth in Vienna,
her escape from the Nazis:
"Freud, I think, was on the train –
I saw him in his carriage.
He was ill, of course, und old,
almost as old as Kedar,"
(she looks towards her husband)
"but *then* Kedar was forty,
und I was a slim young girl.
Ach, who would believe it now!
When Kedar brought me back here
I weighed no more than eight stone.
Our patients used to bring food –
food for *me* – to the clinic!"

She shakes with coughing laughter,
lights another cigarette,
and waddles between the plants
to refill my empty glass.
"For you I order a crate
next time the man makes a trip,"
she says. "He travels by night,
often his lorry breaks down,
und he wants cash in advance.
But he is reliable,
for an Indian."
I smile,
and thank her. New to the place,
I'm content to say little
among these shrewd denizens.
I watch a camel plod past
on the dusty, dimly lit
main road beyond the garden's
foaming bougainvillaea.

At the *pan*-stand five young men
are discussing in English
the lives of Hindi filmstars.
Their voices, like the harsh cries
(is that a Brain-Fever Bird?)
farther away, sound clearly
in my ears – as though carried
on some element other
than the humid, diesel-fume-
and-incense-heavy night air.
    Mr Modi is telling
the latest bit of gossip
about the Vice-Chancellor's
well-known clandestine *affaire*
with the Princess's sister.
Soon everyone is laughing.
    "Such a nice chap – but a fool,"
our hostess says.
                        Her husband
is murmuring to himself.
He raises his head, his voice
strengthening with the movement.
Incomprehensible words
tumble from his withered lips.
    "These are ancient Sanskrit texts,"
our hostess tells me. "Kedar
has always studied Sanskrit."

    The guests have all stopped talking.
They smoke, or sit with bowed heads
in deferential silence.

The old voice climbs to a chant.
The closed eyes look to the sky.

"He is singing Vedic Hymns,"
she tells me in a whisper.
"Soon we will put him to bed."

A Recovery

The sun bleached out the sky's blue
to a blank page, airily asserting
absence of message: nothing to say.

Everything around me took the hint
and began to shut up. First the shouting,
blossomy bushes hesitated, and grew faint;

then bazaar, crowd, heat, dust, road
refused any more to be self-descriptive,
and cancelled what they'd already said.

As if my brain had suffered a blood-seep,
I walked all day through a world furtive
with secrets – meanings it would not let slip.

    ★   ★   ★

Now evening's turned candid, these purples bold
to assure me of their silhouette-holdings,
their smoke-scarved reaches familiarly filled.

Some *sadhus* are washing an elephant by firelight
in a tree-cloistered *baug*. Wet trunk upcurling
the pleased beast bellows with all its might.

Missionaries in the Hills

Snail-faced religious men from New Zealand
plot against Siva in the big house
five hundred feet above the bazaar.
Their pale blue eyes are missing counters
from a small child's spoiled game.

I pass them every day on the mountain road,
where their sisters and female cousins from Denmark
live in the other house – the bungalow.
They are always cold, those overweight women
who dream of Christ and sticking to diets.

Flute-notes carry far: some things thrive
between green *khud* and green *khud*.
The heart should measure its emptiness
against such flying spaces.
My mind clings to unlikely herbage

scrabbling to stay God-like: imagining
a silversmith's hammer beating thoughts
into fine, hard, lasting designs
fit for a great dancer's ankle,
or the nose-ring of a hill-wife.

Either. Stinks, perfumes, mercantile shades
barricade the exposed town,
so that staring distances can hardly see in.
The crippled beggar sits in his misery's
windowless cell. Around him alleys

soon secrete their bold destinations
in garbage heaps by blind walls,
and in incense-stale cafés. Here days
move slowly, balanced like coolie-loads
edging a route around new land-slips –

no way of hurrying them. The clouds move faster
sightlessly downward: beasts browsing
precipitous slopes, seeking better pastures.
I watch them graze, humpbacked, below –
horizontal flocks in mid-air

dawdling across the plains. Ganga glints
down there in the flat unfocus of heat
and drifting dung-smoke – a silver thread
some few miles sacred from Vishnu's toe,
and charged already with foul wastes.

At this altitude water tumbles clear-voiced:
a hill-dialect I don't understand,
poverty-pure, never written.
The afternoon sickle moon owns nothing
but her dim sibling's slightly squashed face.

Night comes strangely, creeping upward from the depths.
The cold, fat women sing evening hymns.
Hills rear black: spirits of the place
wink like fireflies on their cancelled detail,
dancing in ecstasy at inhuman speed.

★   ★   ★

The Summer House

The Danube glitters and toils
just beyond the walnut trees.
The Great Writer sits at ease
among blooms and disciples.

A garden with an old man –
younger men drinking his wine;
his voice is slow and benign,
the others pause to listen.

When he has nothing to say
he smiles, and sniffs a pink rose
that straggles near his nose.
Sometimes he closes one eye.

His wife, in her painting-smock,
serves us hors d'œuvres and titbits.
She bustles about, then sits
to chatter and have a smoke.

How idyllic, how humane!
I think, testing the thought: –
for such scenes are dearly bought
when foreign troops ring a town.

Betrayals, maybe, and lies
earned them a peaceful old age;
chewing lox I try to gauge
the character of each face.

But I don't know the language,
and they're all strangers to me.
Everybody looks guilt-free,
sunlit near the water's edge.

I included, it must be,
as I stare at the old man
like some homage-heavy fan
silenced by proximity.

Calmed by thoughts that I too wear
the double-dealer's false face,
I begin to like the place,
and move out from my corner.

With the interpreter's help
I talk of Art in the West
for a charming poet-guest
who downs vodka at a gulp.

7

from Metamorphic Adventures
(1996)

Mike and Mae

for Evelyn MacDonald

He the South, and she the North,
Catholic and Protestant
sitting by our English hearth.
Uncompromisingly blunt
in spurning each other's worth,
they seemed in their element

to the boy I was at ten –
ignorant of the Irish
and all the rest. But they'd own
nothing shared, no common crèche:
she called him a "bog-buffoon",
he swore she was churlish –

and hypocritical too!
Only the insults come back,
and brogue ground-bass of the row
I never understood: Mike
all musical from Wicklow,
Mae with her Belfast squawk.

She was "in service" nearby,
my mother's fond underling;
he lodged in our house – though why
he lingered on through bombing
in that Lancashire city
none of us had an inkling.

Mike was good to me: he'd give
me his chocolate coupons
sometimes. He taught me to dive
at the public baths. And once
he took me for a long drive
in one of his firm's blue vans.

Mae I didn't like so much:
her false teeth made clicking sounds.
She demanded that I snitch
on some window-breaking friends.
She walked with a waggling slouch.
She ate my Christmas almonds.

It all seemed fixed for ever –
a permanence guaranteed
by the squabble that never
ended or came to a head
right through one wartime winter
across our hob's shining lead.

Then Mike (or Michael Sean Grey,
as the Inspector called him)
was gone. Police came that day
and tore apart his bedroom:
they said he was IRA
as dangerous as they come.

Mae crowed with self-righteousness –
she'd never trusted the man!
Her false teeth clicked as pious,
patriotic phrases ran
like spittle from her mean mouth.
I loathed her with a passion.

Then she was gone, too: across
the water to a father
dying of a slow disease.
Ireland shrank back to blather
on the air – Jimmy O'Dea's
comedy songs and patter –

and to that Irish absence:
a man with seldom a name
among my mother's dark hints
as she polished the hob's gleam
and turned aside my questions
about our lopsided home.

At St Vincent de Paul Place

for Annamaria Basile

"How did Eddie Frisco die?"
I enquire of Sister Jill,
as she coarse-chops celery
with a thoughtlessly cheerful
expression on her smooth face.

I picture a drunken brawl,
convulsions, or cirrhosis,
and drop the wormy apple
I'm peeling into the tub
with all the other rejects.

Sister fingers her earlobe
gently, assembling the facts –
but, no: her eyes are on Dave,
who's muttering at the sink
about women and lost love,
while his unseeing hands plonk
stacked dishes – an avalanche –
into the soapy water.
Sister walks out from the bench
and touches his hunched shoulder,
telling him to go and eat,
then she steers him through the door
into the dining room's rout.

For a moment I'm left there,
alone in the bright kitchen,
upraised, blunt knife in one hand,
other hand slow-reaching in
among donated Cortlands –
a sorry, bruised, basketful.

Brother Paul enters, paddling
his huge bulk along with small
wrist-movements. "I'm never wrong,"
he says, "good meat-balls can't fail
to please in weather like this!"
Using a ladle, he tastes
the simmering pea soup he's
making for tomorrow. "Just
right!" he says, smacking his lips,
"what would they do without me!"
His squeaky giggles collapse
as Sister Jill walks calmly
across to her chopping board
and takes up where she left off,
as if nothing had occurred.

I have had more than enough
of my task: the few apples
that aren't entirely wormy
or rotten, require careful
sculpting before I can free
their good bits for kitchen use –
and I can't find a sharp blade.
Still, I volunteered for this
particular chore: I should
stick at it till it's finished.

Ten past one. Now Skeet arrives,
flinging off his topcoat, flushed
with manic initiatives.
Sister quietens him down:
soon she has him scouring out
a pasta-encrusted pan –
although his legs and big feet
jog-trot and sidle strangely,
as if fretting to move on
to new opportunity.

Then, suddenly, there's action
on every side, as lunch ends
and help invades the kitchen –
raucous voices, clumsy hands:
Red Fred, a Puerto Rican
with a wall eye, a black guy,
two women dressed like male freaks
and Nancy, who used to screw
Hopalong C and Tom Mix
in her Hollywood heyday.
Washing, drying, carrying,
stacking, they get in the way
of one another's work, sling
friendly insults back and forth
and create such a loud din
that Skeet leaves, with a mild oath,
and Brother Paul – veteran
of many kitchen campaigns –
retreats to the storeroom, where
cans, packages and cartons
stand ranked in silent order.

And there goes the last apple –
straight into the "reject" tub!
I stir the modest panful
of salvaged pieces, the job
finished, except for a few
more long squirts of lemon juice.
Now I must be on my way,
up the hill to my office:
I'm expecting a student
keen to discuss a story
she's written, and I wouldn't
mind a good cup of coffee
before our meeting. Sister's
preoccupied on the phone,

(finger in her other ear
against the room's commotion)
so I nod to the black guy,
skirt the uproar round the sink
and leave without a Goodbye.

On Main Street, a bearded drunk
reels from the Arrawani,
shouting something about God,
and I'm back with Eddie Frisco –
ignorant of how he died
but picturing him anew: gnarled,
hairy; homeless no more. Dead.
His one motto: FUCK THE WORLD
tattooed on his grimed forehead.

Two Memories of Marriage

for Frances

A Provocation

I was kneeling by the grate,
building our earliest fire,
when you crept up on cats' feet
and with one swift motion poured
a jugful of cold water
over my prim composure.

Ah, those were honeymoon days,
when ravenous love and hate
subverted civilities!
I glared through dripping wet
and blustered of rough justice
the next time you dared try it.

Then did nothing of the sort,
being phlegmatic and shy,
and in awe of your upstart
wifeliness – a new country
where I was lost and found out,
poured on and blessed with blue sky.

State I earned banishment from –
but that's a more sombre tale.
Now, I salute our first home,
and praise your ungentle rôle
in fostering the freedom
that forced me into exile.

An Early Death

Our first child was in your womb.
I whispered shy endearments
for hours in the dark bedroom,
and still you lay in a trance

of familial sorrow,
face turned from me to the wall.
Your mother's death was a chill
on the summer air. Moonglow

fingered a patch of carpet
abstractedly. I drowsed in heat
from your shoulder-blades and met
an old friend, on a retreat

in some occupied country.
He seemed to be a novice,
and spoke in any angry voice
of the venal laity,

the puppet government's bribes:
TVs, cars, easy credit.
Ballet music by Delibes
rose from the orchestra pit

in a theatre of my youth.
I was fifteen, bepimpled,
with a trouser-lump levelled
straight along my bated breath

at the radiant dancer
spinning upon the forestage.
The dream disappeared, and there –
charged with lust and my true age –

I reached for your oven flesh,
forced it gently, clambered on,
and with your mute permission
began a violent, rash,

assault upon dark powers
I could not hope to subdue;
your dry gasps edged towards tears
as I laboured inside you.

And then you fell from the place
my being inhabited;
down down down among the dead
you plunged to lament your loss,

dragging me down dumbfounded
mounted on howling grief,
frightened and unbefriended,
aloof in the thrusting life

that gathered its counter-force
to vomit me up and out,
reborn as a heaving brute,
yet fleshless among the stars.

I studied your tear-glazed face,
your lean belly's new hillock –
as if from the depths of space
I were finding a way back

to marriage and birth and death,
earth's daily, small happenings:
I glimpsed our thrown-off night things –
floor-strewn tangles, moonlit cloth –

and took your face in my hands,
kissed mouth, cheek, nose, each eyelid,
then soothed you with loving sounds –
or that's what I hope I did.

Aftermath

Slumped in a prickly armchair
on a humid summer night,
I listened dully to dogs
barking with brainless pleasure
far away and in this street
under the Victory flags.

The bronze eagles with spread wings,
flightless on walls and porches,
reflected the light from stars,
as my slow imaginings
moved between foreign corpses
and these Stars and Stripes of ours.

Sweaty, itching, impotent,
I scratched my shirtless shoulder
and reached for another beer –
like a listless President
dreaming a new world order
from idle thoughts and hot air.

Or like someone long inured
to the crafted, public lies
that lull the popular mind
into easy disregard
for the coarse realities
of imperial command.

The Heroes were coming home –
but not to me in my chair
dogged by barks and disarray;
"Welcome!", the flags flapped, "Welcome!
you fought for all we hold dear
in the mighty USA."

from Some Metamorphic Adventures

Light Fading from a Window

Questions were asked of my head,
my heart, liver, thighbones, feet,
I was ready and eager
to answer them truthfully.

But the sky buzzed with bombers,
the house toppled around me,
and all my eloquent parts
settled finally as soot
in a vast desolation.

From which, reconstituted –
after a stubborn fashion
familiar to my kind –
I began my long journey
in search of the oracle
who had looted my answers.

Distances grew different,
it was a new form of peace,
the signposts had all been changed,
and citizens looked through me
or ran away in terror
as I walked passed their ruins
seeking my destination.

I looked for my resemblance
in still water, polished stones,
and entered a stranger's skull –
a sweating fever-vision,
a hashish-trance where grim gods
spun in high-ringing darkness.

These ominous sequelae
of my childhood diseases
convinced me that my answers
belonged with the oracle –
unless I could learn her mouth.

I rented this lonely room
where it is always evening.

Here I shall practise riddles
in lean, ever-fading light.

Slight Agitations of Leaves

In the annexe of desire
I was favoured among men.
As long as I waited there
a spirit singled me out
for sweetmeats and massages.

The summons was soft music –
then they escorted me in,
lifting my five wits from me
like confiscated weapons.

Sniggering fatuously
I unharnessed my manhood,
granting it freedom at last.

It gave the Commencement Speech
at the College of Babies.

Terrible Mother applauded.

Time to run, I realized,
but machines of flesh gripped me.

Hairy torture-implements
squoze and pulled and gouged and sucked
agony from ecstasy.

They returned my belongings
outside the door marked EXIT,
and threw me into a trench,
bruised, broken, dislocated.

That was a long time ago.
Now the maggots amuse me

who pull my star-chariot
among the far galaxies,
tickling me to sleep at night.

Rain Stains on a Bedroom Wall

I lived in a world of holes,
horrified by orifices.

Each hole was a direct route
to another universe
and a love beyond measure.

My mentors despaired of me.
My mother and father wept
at my wild-eyed blubberings,
my catatonic trances.

Such large luxuries of peace
accompanied my childhood –
unrecognized fragrances
masquerading as stenches.
I did not know my own luck.

War came through all holes at once,
shattering my solid fear,
turning me into a ghost –
a connoisseur of absence.

I could wander where I pleased
in search of universes
and a love beyond measure.

War raged round me silently
as I found and found nothing.

Acorns Falling, Crows Flying

When I arrived home at last
I found the Great House transformed
into a training centre
for foreign mercenaries.
Sentries stood at the west gate,
the enemy's comic flag
flew above the cupola.

I brooded in the shadows
under our family oak,
watching the house neutrally
while cows huddled behind me.
My sphygmomanometer
gave me a sky-high reading.

Of my precious possessions
all lay on the ocean's floor
except for this instrument.
But were my *spirits* soaring? –
that was what I wished to know.

Time was when I understood
social justice and myself.
Not now, after twenty years
in the Empire of Women.

As for the Empress's words –
I couldn't remember them,
just as she had predicted.

Instead, I thought of her love:
death-kisses, tomb-embraces.

What else to rise again from?

Hypochondria remained:
her love-bites seethed and festered.

From one so venereal
might I not have contracted
something far more serious?

Vestigial silliness
punctured by falling acorns.
I read my Statement again,
adjusting a phrase or two.

Now my purpose seemed crazy,
my credentials dubious:
why should the warring factions
accept a mediator
reborn from a royal bed?

I wanted to laugh, or cry,
but couldn't make up my mind
which was more appropriate.
Had I been duped by women? —
the Great House was fading fast,
crows flying through its phantom.

I knew that this was the end:
my sphygmomanometer
registered double zero,
and in a flashback I relived
the storm-tormented shipwreck
as a verse in a ballad
I read a long time ago.

Spoiled Meadows with Some Females

I dissipated my youth
in earnest conversations
with women I didn't know,
and cannot now remember.

The soapworks were so fragrant,
the future so expansive!
O what were we talking of
on those Arcadian walks
through ruined northern landscapes?

Question without an answer –
and more silences appear,
like abandoned, part-drained ponds
among broken brick buildings,
smoky with the sullen glow
that fills a vale at twilight.

Everything shrank as night fell.
Perspectives shrivelled inward.
The women had things to do,
or disappeared abruptly –
but improbable dwarf cries
from the mental hospital
accompanied me homeward.

Such loneliness repelled me.
I sat in the back bedroom
picturing kinder places,
more frivolous encounters,
while soot settled like flawed snow
on the decaying city.

Later, in high palaces,
in temples, hanging gardens,
the past became an odour
pungent and not unpleasant,
as of a nearby bazaar.

So I grow older, at ease
with my half-forgotten youth,
happy in my small knowledge
of this mountainous kingdom.

Bright Birds Squawking Among Vines

Playing on a dismal shore
I made versions of my life –
labyrinth-castles of sand
for the tide to wash away,
with me locked in a dungeon.

The sun's cyclopean eye
stared down through sweltering air
at the nearby salt marshes,
pointedly ignoring me.
I knew I was a watched man.

Being neither young nor old
nor anything in-between,
I thought myself space-fallen –
yet I remembered dimly
an ancient parental smile.

I don't know how much time passed,
or what I was waiting for
in that place where nothing changed.
Hot days followed by hot nights!
Hot nights followed by hot days!

Then, out from the jungle's edge
an emissary stumbled,
pin-cushioned with black arrows,
dying of ticks and snake-bites –
he had come to take me home.

On his corpse I found a map
and explicit instructions
penned in a parental hand.
I strode into the jungle,
glad to be reclaimed at last.

Death came somewhere on the way,
in a malarial dream –
my father's house deserted:
doors flapping, hot wind blowing
through many empty mansions.

Nutritious Meals at Midday

Lunatics and layabouts
adopted me as their friend.

I was praised for idleness
and possession of powers
many gods would have envied.

At the same time my habits
excited the attention
of government officials
studying reams of print-out.

Ignorant and unconcerned,
I carried on as usual
communing with the long-dead
and – every once in a while –
yawning extravagantly.

My language was temperate
in those far-off days of youth.
I drank in moderation,
and even in dreaming flight
greeted with grave politeness
the worst of my enemies.

Yet I did not know the worst:
bullets began to arrive –
as if shot from a rifle –
they ruined a rapt séance
and crippled my best client.

It was downhill from then on:
the police arrested me
for inciting violence.
My ID self-destructed.

Word reached me from the next state
that a male using my name
was performing miracles.

A government impostor,
they said at the soup kitchen.

I played cards in a corner.

Bouts of Love in Bad Weather

I took flight among flowers
and aerial blossomings.
Chatoyant blooms big as clouds
escorted me on my way.
I soared above fragrant banks
with blue earth a blur below.

Closing my eyes I pictured
my eluded only life:
a nothingness at each end,
and between – flubbed rehearsals,
hints of a grand finale.

Theatrical posturings
deserving no rich reward,
yet I glided curvingly
in silent felicity.

Among splayed gleams, thunder-glares,
pollen hollows, underglows –
unfolding into a god.

Or an eternal flower
at the very heart of space.

Who could maintain this for long?
Back in my faded armchair
I belched and shook a numb foot.

Next thing, the door burst open
and my strong-willed landlady
swept the vase from the table
with a cry of "Verboten!"

I gathered the scattered blooms,
drew myself to my full height,
and left immediately
for the Bridge of Suicides –
determined to end it all.

The beautiful floral gift
bestowed by my belovèd
breasted the fog before me.
At the closely guarded bridge
I saw the secret police
apprehending the river.

Children Bouncing Up and Down

I went in pursuit of love.

The route lay through dark tunnels
and wide, cloud-obsessed landscapes.

After a while the terms changed
for no apparent reason:
now all was subtle word-play.

My trekking skills were useless,
my compass acted strangely.
I needed a thesaurus
and a pack of sharper wits.

Nothing was simple enough:
clear meanings echoed wildly,
like clanging, dissonant bells
announcing a great man's death
or the end of a long war.

Such fancies changed to a bed
where I lay survivor-like,
awaiting the arrival
of a Goddess of Wisdom.

Instead a shrew tumbled in
trailing snotty-nosed children
who bounced on me screaming "Dad!"

I didn't give up my quest,
though pinned down for some aeons

by affectionate bodies.

Prophecies and a Closet

The days I expected death
were overcast and heavy
with guilts I could not deny.
Glimpses of eternity
flashed through my head like migraines,
my hot tongue froze at the root,
my cold heart flamed with boredom.

Whether to force the issue
was a question I toyed with
till I forgot what it meant.
Women no longer charmed me
with fluent nature-babble,
nor men with brusque politics.

Yet I grew more popular
as my patience fragmented
into broadcasts of silence:
lost battles brought rejoicing,
my dwindling exploits laughter.

In private I presided
over a bitter household
where everybody suffered
from whitlows and friendlessness.

Thus it was that I succumbed
to clairvoyants' prophecies
concerning my secret nights
as the club-footed lover
of impossible women,

and when the Capitol fell
(pluming slow-motions of dust
crawled through by troops with guitars!)
the Assistant Director
found me in a clothes-closet
meditating on Nothing.

This trumped-up drama soon palled:
I preferred reality,
or something approaching it,
even though my back teeth ached
with displaced anxieties.
I wrote it all in a book:
"The Tale of a Human Life".

Towards a Sulking Spirit

In some old war or bar-fight
I had been badly wounded:
my left leg was inches short,
one of my eyes was missing.

Still, I remained vigorous
for a man so handicapped,
shopping daily for my needs,
attending lectures on Art
at notable museums.

Women thought me intriguing.
My hip-swivelling hobble
and silken, paisley eye-patch
often led to coy questions
concerning the full extent
of my private injuries.

I found it necessary
with certain forward beauties
to prove my manhood intact
in the most obvious way –
thus satisfying all doubt
and incurring the expense
of five paternity suits.

Number six was in the works
when I became bedevilled
by nightmares of infamy:
my wounds were self-inflicted –
I had crippled my young self
to avoid National Service!

Were these dream-scenes true or false?
The genie who brought me wealth,
my wise and trusted servant,
wouldn't answer the question.
He sulked, deep in his bottle.

And mother was no better:
once again she assured me
that she remembered nothing
of my birth, childhood and youth.

         ★   ★   ★

Caterpillars

They descended on filaments so fine
you could see them only with narrowed eyes,

against the mottling of afternoon
sun and shine and leaf-backs and shadows.

And they themselves were well camouflaged:
slimy, hairy or powdery-dry,

their dangling, suckered crawliness smudged
leaf-like into the quivering greenery.

Yet nothing deceived our hunting skill:
matchboxes at the ready, we stood

watching them drop in jerky, spiral
motions until they were safely stowed

under the signs of Captain Webb,
Swan Vestas, Puck and England's Glory.

There, cropping titbits of grass and herb
we'd stuck in the boxes, small mouths made rubbery

munching noises – or so we assured
one another, each tight-shut box held close

to the whorls of a summer-grubby ear,
in the cool blue space beneath the branches.

Then the day went wrong: pushes, squabbles,
boxes snatched and contents tipped out –

squashed underfoot, so that yellow entrails
were all we had to show for our effort.

I wonder what happened next? No matter.
There we go – galloping out of sight,

a righteous posse: ignorant centaurs
slapping rough thighs in the sooty sunlight.

Broughton Sonnets

for Lowell Svensen

I

Suffer the little children to come unto me
was the first thing we saw when the door was open,
and the blond, blue-eyed man with kids on his knee,
framed above the text, in a reproduction.
A teacher played a sprightly piano tune:
around the room we marched in our Sunday best –
except for Mrs Jackson's mongoloid son,
who shuffled straight to his chair, like an honoured guest.

Jesus, with a fixed, magnanimous stare,
smiled at his kids – he never looked at us
as we passed and passed before his holy face;
it was Billy who took us all into account,
following us around from his scraping chair,
his puffed face rapturously vacant.

2

Dust smells, disinfectant, varnished pine,
inadequate lighting and an air of gloom
offered to us the church's invitation
to form a youth club, and to feel at home
among stacked chairs and broken furniture
on nights when functions didn't grace the hall:
our dead-dull spirits quickened at the lure
of something different – anything at all!

So in we came from lamplit-corner lounging
to virtuous boredom, records, cups of tea,
where wakeful dreams of what comes after kissing
would not be put down by Monopoly,
nor by the skidding drives with which we trounced
opponents when their looping flatshots bounced.

3

Except when injured, or with sudden hurts,
one didn't talk about one's hidden parts,
and so throughout my childhood I supposed
that I was *ritually* circumcised
and thus was sort-of Jewish, like the boys
I got on best with – all of whom were Jews:
Waxman, Eisenberg, Adler, Joey Aaron
(though playground cricket was our shared religion).

By adolescence, lighting shabbes-fires
for Yiddish-speaking, wealthy foreigners,
I knew that I was thorough English-gentile,
whose oddness – hidden, undiscernible –
was secret as the poetry I wrote,
fingering my foreskin's absence late at night.

4

A synagogue, a mikvah and a kheydr
gave to our street a special character:
exotic, problematic, with a hint
of something formlessly recalcitrant,
not only in the yarmulkes and beards,
the chicken-barley smells, the foreign words,
but in the snot-nosed, ragged gentile kids
who muttered – like their parents – "dirty yids!"
Listening, gawping there, my soul went sullen,
obscure with prejudice and admiration,
then skulked among a maze of alleyways
for years, affectionately treacherous –
the puzzled, covert enemy of friends
and impotent imaginer of broken bounds.

5

Philip, Lord Wharton, died aged eighty-three
in sixteen ninety-six, but not before
he'd willed the income from some property
to purchase Bibles for the virtuous poor –
children who could commit to memory
those psalms his Lordship thought beyond compare.
Trustees conveyed his grave philanthropy
down through the years, until it reached our Claire –
the little sneak! She studied on the sly
then winsomely recited, word for word,
six psalms, to win a Bible at first try,
while dry contestants rolled their eyes and "er-ed",
and I – who would have bettered her, if present –
kept in the dark, played cricket on the Crescent.

6

My cousin Winnie's wobbly-pitched soprano
fluttered above the choir – an injured bird –
whether she sang with others, or sang solo;
and worse than that, she talked about "Our Lord"
as if he were her boss at the Prudential,
and she his ever-willing invoice clerk!
I often thought that I'd rather be sinful
than tone-deaf good, and pious about work.
Still, she had faith – and talent of a sort
(the choir-master praised her to the skies),
and I was faithless, with an empty heart,
the nasty smiler in a crowd of boys
less snide than I, and better – no one else
brutalized wit to sublimate such ills.

7

My mother made no bones about the crimes
that sent John Connor running, with the police
hot in pursuit. Among her constant themes:
his sly deceits, his cruel and crooked ways –
embezzlement, fraud, the bilking of little people,
the secret jeers at those who'd trusted him.
She kept him distantly contemptible,
although it didn't strike me at the time.

Later, I thought he'd stirred her sexual guilt
then left her stewing in it. Later still,
I thought he'd soured her with the cunning tricks
by which he got her pregnant by a Celt –
she of the true-blue pride and iron will,
who hated Irishmen and Catholics.

8

God never startled me with revelation
or even crept up quietly on my heart
as I was nodding through some high-flown sermon,
dully aware of how my buttocks hurt.
Nor did he live among the park's green acres,
the air-raid shelter's dungeon-stink of piss;
bonfires, rockets, pin-wheels, cracker-jackers
blazed with a glorious power that was not his.

I scorned to pray: I knew he'd done a bunk
when I was five, to whereabouts unknown.
His absence was the church I worshipped in:
a secret silence, fetid, growing rank
in every face I didn't recognize,
in every blank stare at my searching eyes.

An Unhappy Soul

In Memoriam R.P.

From the first time he sought me out
I knew he was troubled. He cracked his knuckles,
and tossed meaninglessness about
in long poems he dragged like shackles

wherever he went. His eyes shot flares
from something in distress, and foundering;
he soon tried to push me downstairs,
while I was still naïve, and wondering

what satisfaction he thought he'd find
in having me as his acquaintance:
I think he needed one of his kind,
but free – as it seemed – from his harsh sentence.

Sometimes he'd weep with drunken love,
sometimes he'd drool out sullen hatred
like stinking ectoplasm. "Enough!"
I'd shout – from uneasy selfhood battered

by accusations I knew from dreams,
as often hurled by my own demons.
His conversation, poor in themes,
was rich in dark hints, and disastrous omens.

And now he is dead, his ex-wife writes:
run down on a country road in Flintshire,
by a person unknown, one dark midnight –
the coroner's verdict: *Misadventure.*

I'd long since banished him from my life,
stopped writing him cheques and recommendations;
he'd threatened me with more than a knife,
more than his failures, more than unruly passions.

So I ought to be glad to know for sure
that never again will he ever find me:
that I'll never meet him at my door,
or turn to see him scowling behind me;

but I harbour the fear that, body-free,
his painful spirit, ever-seeking
impossible balm, will light on me
and settle in my house, sour and grave-mocking.

George Lee and Apprentice

for Edwina Trentham

They brought him back under mild duress
from pottering in his rose garden
to painting the blooms he knew so well.

Most of the young were in the forces
and his generation dead and gone,
so in he came – grumbling at recall,

slur-footed, weak-eyed, cheerfully querulous –
every day at about eleven
to practise the lifetime's craft and skill

he thought he'd said goodbye to. The boss
told me to help him; pay attention
to his needs, and learn from his example

as a Master Designer. I was all eyes
and ears and attitudes of devotion;
but he couldn't abide this gawping, soulful,

supplicant at the throne of his genius:
"Fetch me a cup of tea and a bun,"
he said, "and then get hold of yon pestle

and mortar, and I'll demonstrate how us
old 'uns grind colour. Off you go, son –
and don't bring me a bun that's stale!"

I learned how to fetch and carry, my face
less spotty, it seemed, now I was certain
of one small thing; my heart in less turmoil

now that the old man softened his voice
in affectionate teasing: "Oh, *that's* your opinion! –
too deep for me, lad, too intellectual."

For months I was the humblest apprentice,
mixing pigments with smelly gum,
cleaning his brush, sharpening his pencil,

tidying his cluttered working space.
Then, one foggy, darkening noon,
he donned his Homburg, threw down his maul-

stick with a thump, and said, "Bugger this –
I'm catching the 62 to Chorlton
before they stop running! Show me your mettle:

I've painted the main motif – bouquets
and ribbons. You complete the design.
Do all the repeats, horizontal and vertical,

and make it everywhere look seamless,
as if one hand had worked in unison
with a single brush. Copy my style,

in other words. Goodbye. God bless!"
He lurched away, slammed the door, and was gone.
So there I stood, beside his easel,

pleased by his trust, yet awed; and nervous
to prove of myself a good craftsman,
even though I was sure I wouldn't fail.

It took me hours and hours of close
attention and stuck-out tongue to fashion
colourful blooms in full petal

from the old man's rubbed-down graphite trace
of arthritic, instructive, spider-outline;
and then the ribbon – shining like foil –

that looped and twisted in luscious curlicues
across the trellised ground of fawn
to touch the roses and there entangle!

For the first time I felt all-of-a-piece,
as I made and watched the scattered design
cohere in all its parts, until

it covered the stretched paper and froze
in final form: the specious perfection
of one man's gift, bold and inimitable.

Then the caretaker arrived, an officious
complainer: everyone else had gone;
I should have left at five – it was a rule!

I shuffled homeward, fog on face,
tentative, outstretched hand fog-hidden;
my spirit eager, clear-eyed, bountiful,

striding among exotic vistas
where bunting flapped and the sun shone –
as if it were holidaying at Blackpool.

Whether the old man made a fuss
over my work, saying, "Well done,
lad, you deserve a putty medal!"

or whether he found my detail careless,
my touch unworthy of his tuition,
I cannot recollect at all.

I know that he gave me other chances
to complete designs he had begun,
and that by degrees I became responsible

for more and more. Those were Victory days
of returning, sunburned young men and women,
with tales to tell, hopes to fulfil.

And I, too, was full of high purpose:
a neophyte artist, longhaired, wan,
attending evening classes at art school.

I saw myself as above the atelier's
service to glazed chintz, rep and linen,
to businessmen and the industrial

giant which paid my measly wages.
I meant to outpaint Augustus John,
Turner, Fuseli, Burne-Jones, Constable,

and scorned the old man's patient largesse
as tricks of a trade I viewed with disdain:
the enemy of Art and the Spiritual.

By the time he grunted "Bugger this! –
I'm off back to my bloody garden!"
I'd shifted my stool to join a cabal

of newly demobbed designers, whose
tales and mutterings of rebellion
against the firm assumed me as their equal.

I hadn't the mind to take much notice
of the old man's putting his street-clothes on
and raising his hat in mute farewell

to work and us and the sketched-in dahlias
he'd never be back to paint full-blown
in cunning repeats, horizontal and vertical.

He had gone for good – which I didn't realize
till I cleared his board of that last design
a week or so later. His wonky easel,

maul-stick and brushes I claimed for my own use.
The rest of his mess went into the dustbin
when a younger man was assigned to his desk and stool.

On the San Andreas Fault

for Stan James

The hippie, Jewish-Buddhist anorexic,
creeping about the house on dirty feet
when she wasn't chanting mantras, stole a pack
of Camels from the bags I hid too late.

"Not that she smokes," explained the paid companion
of the hippie's wealthy grandma (who owned the house):
"she steals because her father was a stuntman,
buried before she learned to know his face,

and Hollywood claimed her mother for a starlet –
that unloved child was raised in foster-care!
Padlock your bedroom door and watch your wallet,
whatever's missing you must blame on her."

The paid companion followed Krishnamurti;
the wealthy grandma – nearly eighty-six –
did Music Meditation with a Sufi
while sipping Scotch, which helped her to relax.

I smiled and chatted, glad to be a house-guest –
yet with my soul's left eyebrow cocked askance,
as if I were an unacknowledged fascist,
the northern enemy of southern nonsense –

then strode the chaparral, the fire-bald mountains,
the avocado and the orange groves,
accompanied by my old Lancastrian phantoms,
touting their cautious, parsimonious lives.

And when I found a crucifix in a tangle,
clumpy with mud and pebbles on the beach,
I teased it out, watered it free of shingle,
and hung it round my neck like a reproach,

a something ... but my thoughts turned Californian,
vague as the hazy oil-rigs out at sea
beyond the surfer rapt upon his Helicon
of arching water's small eternity.

A Picture of R.C. in a Prospect of Blossom

In the still, warm air of afternoon
you stand beneath the magnolia tree
watching the blossoms fall. Your face
upturned is secret as the moon,
bland in the blue, though hours too soon.
A petal descends with deathly grace,
another lies on your arm, I see.

It is your eleventh spring, and yet
your first – because you feel it so:
never before such scents to smell,
never such drenching slippery sweat,
such birdsong, or such flowers to pet.
You run from the house (whose wintry spell
still mutters of storms and ice and snow)

to skip barefooted on the grass,
or jump from favourite stone to stone,
or else sit solemn on the stoop
watching the link-arm lovers pass –
as if they held some magic glass
in which came shimmering into shape
scenes of your future fully grown.

And now what silent reverie
holds you with bated thought and breath
beneath the surprising moon, among
the flakes of blossom still breaking free
and the fallen abundance of the tree?
I see you standing statue-strong
and tiptoe-deep in brilliant death.

8

Poems 1996–2005

for Michael de Larrabeiti

Kitchen Work

To give a dull day meaning
I set radishes draining,
upright on a chopping board,
unnatural and absurd
as their extravagant dew
from the supermarket's spray.

Each balanced on its lopped end,
they formed a portly, red band
of voiceless vegetables
speaking to human troubles
that stood like ugly heirlooms
in my waking mind and dreams.

I left the counter tableau
and bore my burdens away
on small, everyday errands
to stores, and sensible friends
who'd straighten me out at once,
if I gave them half a chance.

But secrets of the kitchen
told my tongue not to begin:
meaning might brighten the day
when the radishes were dry,
and my heirlooms disappear
in silent, eloquent air.

At Clover Nook

for Lisa Simmons

A bright Sunday afternoon,
two women I am fond of,
who talk of growing children,
marriage, divorce, death, love.
Cats meow to come in, dogs bark,
trees in the yard disperse leaves,
one woman makes a wry joke
about men's hidden motives.
The other, who shares the house,
laughs as she grinds coffee,
then tells of her early days
lap-dancing in Miami –
"Reprehensible, but neat!"
she adds, over her shoulder.
I nibble a cracker and wait
for themes less familiar.

The kitchen is visited
by a teenage malcontent,
who butters a piece of bread,
silently impertinent,
then sidles back whence she came –
the women raise their eyebrows,
like partners in a board-game
based on cheating and false throws.
But soon return to matters
of adult complexity –
J's politics, F's tempers,
and what to do about T?
They ask my opinion,
I offer conflicting thoughts;
one mocks me with affection,
the other echoes my doubts.

And so the afternoon goes,
until I stand at the door
smoking in leafy shadows
beneath new moon and one star,
with the women drinking wine
behind me in the lit house –
their arguments growing keen,
their good humour boisterous.

A Downward Look

The slack-skinned backs of my hands,
rope-veined beneath mottled shine,
won't let me forget old age.
I may bunch fists, to amend
appearances and regain
taut compactness, like a badge
of youth (when I remember
to practise the deception),
but it isn't to fool *me*:
seventy is the number
of my years, lived and gone.
I think of death every day.

Yet, still, I ponder the heft
of living hands – fluent parts
for most of a long lifetime:
agile in love, quick in theft,
a safe pair in certain sports
and useful about the home –
now grown reluctant to stray,
the gauzy-wrinkled, arthritic
servants of an old poet.
Scarecrow memento mori,
one resting on a notebook,
one writing verse across it.

Perhaps they should learn to pray –
come tremblingly together
in dubious travesty
of childhood naiveté,
while I mouth the "Our Father"
or supplicate God's mercy
to spare me a common death?

They – and I – won't posture so:
we've lived here too long, alone –
faithful denizens of earth
in the changing body's slow
fumble towards extinction.

Dental Trouble

Loose teeth and infected gums –
my friend's poor face is swollen.
Yet he smiles (making no claims
on my sympathy), melon-
reminiscent features stretched
to an unlikely limit,
before the smile is dispatched,
and teeth wince away from it.

Saturday: drink-and-talk night.
We're lost in the usual
maze of after-hours deep thought,
though we loll in casual
attitudes of unconcern
on my living room sofas,
discussing the Gates of Horn,
baseball, dentistry, *Slokas*.

Reaching a clearing, my friend
dwells on his new-found woman,
who's kindly and in command.
He views as a good omen
the firm appointment she's made
for him to receive treatment –
dental care he's long delayed,
in bachelor resentment.

But he's past all that. His face
manages to look jolly,
as I drunkenly address
the dream-meaning of *Kali*.
Then he's off to watch a game
starting on television;
I picture his brisk walk home,
puffed face bright with affection.

Forgotten Celebration

There I am, loudly awake,
laughing at somebody's joke,
a well-dressed crowd around me
beneath a blossoming tree.

Could it be a wedding scene –
rice-strewn grass, hors d'œuvres, champagne,
those inward-looking females
hugging their delighted souls?

In the snapshot I've no beard,
my eyes are bright, I'm longhaired
and expansive with primed sex,
circa nineteen sixty-six.

I eke out the plain image,
hoping to give mind a nudge
towards youthful sentience,
rank, full-bodied existence –

that person at whom I stare
as if I were never there.

Junking

Ragged plastic bags flutter
impaled on the barren trees
at the edge of the town dump.
Beyond the trees, the river –
cluttered with sluggish iceflows.
I can't see it from this ramp,
where I've stopped my borrowed truck
to unload broken machines
from my household, but slopping,
lapping, watery sounds sneak
across the foetid silence
of the mountainous shopping-
squalor that looms above me,
making my cowed soul quicken
at the prospect of spring thaws
greening our fertile valley –
flowers in bright bloom again,
summer nights under the stars.

I hold my breath, man-handling
the clapped-out washing machine
across, onto the tailboard,
eyes on the backside – writing
I've not read before, or seen –
a "Specification Card"
with a bold CAUTION below –
then I push the machine off,
to clang and settle beside
a crazily tilting row
of rusty, once-pristine proofs
that Life can be clean and good.

The stink is stifling. I heave
my smaller appliances
onto the rubble-strewn ground,
reverse the truck fast and leave,
past the sewage farm's chimneys.

This is the poor end of town.

Double-Dappled

Beyond the open meadow,
a break in the silhouette
of bordering foliage
brought hands to my dazzled eyes
against low, October light.
Now separate trees stood out,
in variegated greens,
within a luminous shade
alive with wind-blown movement,
and I saw that the tree-break
was grounded in absence –
a gap in dense undergrowth.

Double-dappled with fallen leaves,
shadows and sunlight, a path curved
into the wood and out of sight.
My watch told me to go home,
and listen to breaking news
of the latest, distant war,
but my feet walked me towards
that inkling of a poem
almost, but never written.

The path held for forty yards,
and petered out in brambles,
entangling a few bald tyres,
barbed wire in a loose coil
and pieces of an engine,
roughly wrapped in black plastic.
Not what I had expected,
but not surprising, either –
a farmer's dump: terminus
of a path leading nowhere.

I kicked a tyre, threw a stick
and stood there – an alien,
fluent in the wrong language.
Then I rushed home to listen
to the Pentagon's update.

Late Appearance

I saw your face in a dream:
beauty coarsened by madness.
You wore a dishevelled dress,
an expression of dumb doom.
Our children were running wild,
you took no notice of them;
playing with your dress's hem,
you were the abandoned child.

I stared in belated grief
at your thirty-year-old woe,
from which I stayed far away
and offered no kind relief.
Why must I witness that pain
now your troubled life's over
and I with a new lover
am coming to life again?

A Pair of Gloves

i.m. H. Booth, M.D.

No doubt Humphrey wore these gloves
of tailored, soft, black leather,
to impress his lady-loves
and medical committees.

His sister gave them to me
when we interred his ashes;
Humphrey, dead at fifty-three,
had exhausted his options.

I recall him in his pride,
charismatic, commanding,
a man who postured and lied
as if he were powerless.

In money and mid-career,
surrounded by minions,
he prospered from year to year,
raffish and self-indulgent.

With something of high-class crime
shading his bedside manner:
I pictured him serving time,
or, perhaps, being knighted.

But he avoided disgrace
and was ignored for honours,
as he skipped from place to place,
a vain fool, or a hero.

I gaze at my hands and muse
on all that's left of Humphrey –
these gloves I use and abuse,
doing my late-fall yard work.

Between their scarred palms I shift
branches snapped from the maple;
their wet fingers scoop and lift
heaps of dead leaves for compost.

Strange, that Humphrey, of all men,
should join me in such labours.
I gaze at his gloves again;
they gaze at me like jurors.

With Gus at Guida Farm

The dog goes ahead of me
through the snowy cow-pasture.
Chest-deep, he ambles and lopes,
then stops in a cautious way,
looking back to make quite sure
I'm following in his steps.
Satisfied, he shakes his ears,
back-kicks a little blizzard
from his powerful hind legs,
dashes on and disappears
in bushes, chasing a bird
he'll never catch. My coat snags
on a tangle of bramble,
strewn among path-side creeper –
and jolted branches dislodge
their shelved snow in one big spill,
showering upon my hair
more whiteness, like age on age.
My bad knee begins to ache,
as if in confirmation
of my seventy-one years –
but suddenly the dog's back,
with the world newly begun,
and a stick between his jaws
for me and a throwing game.
I throw, and he proves his breed
as a retriever – over
and over, until I am
stiff armed and he is clotted,
head to tail, with bristly snow.
Then we head for Goose Meadow,
through wind-blown flakes, falling fast.
The far hillside's disappeared
in speckled, curtaining grey
and the dog dims to a ghost

chasing a ghostlier bird
away to my left. I call,
whistle and turn towards home,
limping along old ski-tracks
already too scuffed to spoil –
and the dog bounds past, spuming
snow and first-time frolics.

Fire Wardens

Crossing our warm little town
on a fine October day,
my mind kept running on things
forgotten, or never known,
like Mr Hubbard's reply
to Mr Bloch's misgivings.

Both part of the same story
told to me by Mr Hubbard
far away and long ago.
(I tripped on a present tree,
as I walked, blind and apart,
in a war's heavy shadow.)

Those ill-matched men, both long dead,
arguing over a bomb
unexploded and unlit,
blurred with my later childhood's
hearing of that freak, wartime
patrol from Mr Hubbard,

on a street where a disused
air-raid shelter still loomed
to echo back our footsteps.
(I stopped, rapt and slightly dazed,
hearing myself hailed and named,
among maple leaves in heaps.)

What but fall in New England,
my social-worker neighbour
and a Pin for a Good Cause!
Overhead a biplane droned
peacefully through azure air,
negating my memories

for a second – then I walked
that rainy, Lancashire street
again in my puzzling mind,
a mind that stumbled and baulked
at fully believing what
Mr Hubbard may have dreamed,

or *I* may have dreamed, I thought –
moving right-ward rapidly
to let past rollerbladers –
for the two men never met,
to my knowledge, although I
knew each one as a neighbour.

But Mr Hubbard *had* told
of a long night's firewatching
in Mr Bloch's company,
hadn't he? I stood baffled
by memory and making
mind at duplicitous play.

That atheistic plumber
disputing with the devout,
Jewish refugee florist,
the inertness of a bomb
fallen at their very feet,
in a dark, fire-watchers' tryst! –

what a scene for a movie,
I thought, suddenly certain
I'd made up the entire thing,
or most of it, anyway;
and relieved of the burden
of distrustful witnessing,

I found myself light-hearted
on Main Street and nowhere else,
with a crosslight blinking *Walk*
and not a thought in my head
but coffee and fresh bagels,
where my friends waited to talk.

Alone in the Living Room

Those love-lorn women – phoning
and coming round late at night –
long since succumbed to silence;
I sit distracted, reading.
Do *they* give even scant thought
to their youthful indigence –

in bed beside good husbands,
reckoning household accounts,
placating fractious children?
I recall their wild errands,
gravid with movie-romance
wished on a cold-hearted man

who could not be different
(so charming and so remote),
now, as all those years ago.
Bleak reality blinds print;
the still room gapes, desolate,
as if I needed it so.

The Young Fruiterer

He is accurate and fast
taking the order – bagging
the vegetables and fruits,
guessing what you would like most
to carry home, from among
the coffees, foreign chocolates,
chutneys, biscuits and cheeses
he's added to Goods in Stock,
since he took over the store.
No woman likes him the less
for his fierce zeal to re-make
his role as inheritor
of his dad's dominion,
though some remember fondly
the old man's limp, the vague looks
in search of fruit in season,
the peanuts he gave away,
the hand patting their buttocks.

Haymaking

for Kathleen White

Two old men on old tractors
are collecting bales of hay,
helped by a bevy of boys,
who swing their legs from flatbeds,
and joke around, standing up.

The brothers have worked this field
and the adjacent pastures
for most of their lives. They grazed
dairy cows on these meadows,
until they sold the farmland
to the town, when they retired,
both well over seventy.
The land can't be developed –
that was their stipulation,
dressed in their best suits and ties,
sitting down with the lawyers.
And *they'd* look after the place,
with the right to gather hay
for as long as either lived.

This is the tale I've been told,
and the tale I think about,
as I approach the tractors,
walking the fragrant, mown field,
through the long shadows of trees
on a sunny afternoon
in late fall. I'd like to thank
the old men for the acres
they've turned to Nature Reserve –
but know that I'll stay silent.

Each leans on his steering-wheel —
motionless as his tractor —
while the boys run back and forth,
heaving bales on to flatbeds
with lewd curses and laughter.
Then they jostle back aboard
and the tractors move onward.

I overtake them, at last,
up near the edge of the wood,
a tangle of undergrowth
thorny and thick with berries.
The boys aren't interested
in a greybeard limping along —
they're lost in their workgame — but
the old men nod me a look
of wary recognition.
They may have seen me before,
or is this Mortality
acknowledging its own face?
Who knows. I waggle my stick
upright and leave the brothers
grumbling at the skittish boys,
who hurl the last bales wildly,
and whack one another's butts.

Ahead of me the meadow
stretches unwelcomingly,
in silent, cooling shadow,
and soon I'm on my own again,
where flocks of small, startled birds
rise from stubble, scattering
in rapid, zig-zagging flight.

Snowy Night

Alone in my once-loud house
and restless among white streets
full of one a.m. silence,
from room to room, under lights
illuminating absence,
I drifted with my dry thoughts.

On the desk in the study
an open notebook displayed
words I had thought worth writing;
the living room air echoed
with disputes come to nothing;
the fridge hymned its own cold void.

Climbing to prepare for bed,
I touched the bannister-rail
with uneasy affection.
Returning down the stairwell
I thought of a moist woman
gentling her lover's strong will,

then stared across the dark porch
at the lamp-lit falling snow's
reversals, drifts and eddies –
my dry thoughts all shaken loose,
like shifting snowflake-shadows
each shaped for its certain spouse.

A Marriage Made in the Balkans

I forget that she seemed odd –
too long from flat chest to thighs,
comic accent, tragic eyes –
when she moved among the crowd
in the room where I met her
for the first time. Twelve months on
she lolls on a black futon,
startlingly familiar
in self-evident beauty
and the friendship between us.

She's asked me here to discuss
something in deep secrecy
(her husband's out of town).
She plays with a cigarette,
not ready to tell me yet,
then comes to a decision,
rearranges each striped limb
and says that pretence must end –
she's in love with my old friend,
"You introduced me to him!"

My *new* friend is her husband,
and I feel complicitous,
as well as slightly envious
of these three I've helped to bind
in a tight entanglement
that might enliven them all.
She rises, elegant, tall,
her passion to confess spent –
at least for the time it takes
to bring me another beer –
then she's dabbing at a tear
she feels on her cheek (or fakes).

Wielding her second language,
exiled from a shattered state,
she's domiciled yet remote:
the lost child of privilege.

She tells me at detailed length
of this wonderful *affaire*,
extolling her new lover,
his kindness, his gentle strength.
I picture my dull, old friend
in her exotic embrace;
he's beguiled – and at a loss,
wondering where it will end.
I think of her duped husband,
the drinking companion
I dare not drink with again,
now I'm heavily burdened
with his wife's sweet secret:
the knowledge of his defeat.
But my speech is all deceit,
interested and polite.
And now, again, she seems odd,
lolling opposite my chair,
while I brood upon honour
with every comment and nod.

Jericho and Miss Jones

Knowing it from Sunday School,
in my eight-year-old's fashion,
Jericho – where Miss Jones died –
went tumbling and trumpeted,
its wheeling-overhead sun
stopped by God's suspended rule;

and Joshua stood, arms wide-
raised and mixed-up with Moses
in an old painting I'd seen,
even Jesus in his white gown
and golden beard and tresses
was present at the bedside.

But when my mother told me
that "Jericho" was the name
of the County Town Hospice
where Miss Jones died, cancerous
and alone – no friend to claim
her body, no family –

I felt sad for the person
I'd often seen on our street –
the hurrying, grey hobble,
the false teeth fixed in a smile.
But I knew why I'd first thought
of Sunday School religion

and the tales the teachers read:
they meant more to me than death
and Miss Jones – featureless, blurred,
in a distant cancer ward –
except for her large false teeth,
still smiling on in my head.

In the Health Care Center, Inc.

Dulled by drugs and ninety years,
he doesn't recognize me –
nor is he the man I know
from the end-house on my street –
yet I sidle through flowers,
moving awkwardly past his feet.

I shout into the strange face
good wishes sent by neighbours;
his thin hand cups one deaf ear
and gestures understanding.
Beside the bed, in a glass,
sunken dental plates lie grinning.

Soon he remembers my name
and courteously enquires
of my health and my children.
His strength's increasing each day,
he says – next week he'll be home,
back to his own room and TV.

I smile and shout pleasantries,
mixed with bits of local news;
he recalls touring Devon
and his family's Great House,
back in the nineteen thirties,
when he was single and foot-loose.

Other memories follow.
I bend my face to his lips'
meandering monotone,
but his speech slips into snores,
his mouth assumes a wet O
and I'm left to my own affairs.

Except for the Asian aide,
who bustles in to the man
choking upon a device
beyond the dividing screen.
She heaves him upright in bed,
adjusting his stainless machine.

End of Innocence: 1956

Like a furtive miracle,
that sexual encounter
among her Hostel's bushes!
She, an Australian girl
at the peak of a Grand Tour
with an Englishman, no less,
fucking her way to marriage –
a home in U.K. for good!
I, a tethered mother's boy,
hauled across the prescribed edge
of feathered family bed
into prickly weeds of joy.

Confused more than by Suez
to find myself a virgin
no longer at twenty-eight,
I brushed off elbows and knees,
thinking vaguely of Eden
(who was to broadcast that night)
and the overgrown garden
complete with its awkward Eve
fumbling at pink suspenders.
I stood, eager to be gone,
but rooted like a love-slave
in that victor's look of hers.

Eisenhower refused support,
I remember well enough,
and all her father's fortune,
gleaming around her good heart
in young flesh eager for love
couldn't make marriage happen –

though how I made my escape
doesn't come back to me now.
I know I was at the train
that autumn, watching her weep
as she said her last good-bye,
never to return again.

Old Treasures

Coming across a volume
of Auden's early poems
unopened for many years,
I remembered my first home
and the ill-informed daydreams
guiding my boyish labours.

Inside the volume's cover,
poems clipped from magazines
lay in a brittle, brown sheaf:
poor things I thought fine and rare
when I lodged them near Auden's
as hopeful semblance of proof.

That was a broken-down time,
after the Second World War.
I was awaiting Call-Up,
fumbling with metre and rhyme
in my mother's cold parlour,
working by day at a shop,

and haunting the darkest stacks
of the local library,
where narrow columns of print
leapt from the neglected books
that opened themselves to me —
their long-delayed visitant.

Not that I knew good from bad:
anything with lots of white
around it seemed to contain
dormant magic; shadow-food
for poems I couldn't write,
yearnings I couldn't define.

Which is why I smoothed and tucked
those poor things in with Auden's:
all might sustain me some day,
while I wrote without defect,
cloistered in the sweet gardens
of understood poetry.

Drawing a War Plane

In the middle of the night
mother heard the piano
being played by ghostly hands
downstairs, in the living room.
That was when Dr Bennett
told her to take up smoking
to calm her nerves – and her mind's
whirling thoughts of death and doom.

I heard her telling Aunt Jean,
after a morning air-raid,
the smoke of a Player's Weight
wreathing from between her lips,
as they talked in the kitchen.
Aunt Jean shook her curls and said,
"*He* thinks you've imagined it;
he's all horses and hot tips

and floosies, too, so I've heard.
He wouldn't know a spirit
from a sponge-cake – he's earth-bound,
that's what he is!" "Well, it *was*
her favourite, 'The Lost Chord',"
mother said, "and I *did* shoot
bolt upright as that weird sound
filled every room in the house."

Aunt Jean said, "If you ask me,
Gran's trying to get in touch
with you from The Other Side.
How long's she been gone – six weeks?
Ample time for her to try-
out her new-found powers, such
as returning from the dead
through midnight spirit-music."

Mother's frown was furious.
"Stop talking rubbish!" she said,
"It was nothing but a dream;
since Gran died I've been shook-up,
and these air-raids make things worse."
Aunt Jean almost spoke, then sighed
instead and tried to look grim
over her lifted teacup.

Was I drawing a war plane
at the rickety table,
apparently self-absorbed,
but privy to every word,
while stealing looks now and then
at the women's mild squabble,
fleshy and flowery-garbed,
in front of the sink-cupboard?

I doubt it: my memories
of childhood are not so clear
and detailed. But there I am –
necessarily ensconced
among the inventive lies
the poet told to ensure
the drama of his poem –
silent and yet unsilenced.

Helping Miss May

A humid summer evening.
Heavy trees above the street,
where a half-hidden schoolboy
is clipping his teacher's hedge.

Bright light fades from cooling air.
Snip-snipping blades meet slowly.
The teacher calls the boy in,
to supper on a white cloth.

Books on the shelves all around
ask the boy silent questions.
He eats cold sausage and ham
while the teacher tells him things.

Midnight in Manchester

That wet ride on the last bus
brought me to myself, as if
manhood began to take place
when I noticed the long loaf
sticking like a plump phallus –
braided, varnished and stiff –
from Mr Greenberg's embrace,
where he sat sprawled, nodding off.

How old was I – seventeen?
Bog-eyed with booze and brain-sex,
after a night on the town
drinking among dirty jokes
with Dave and Eddie and John,
I sat there full of dislikes:
for Greenberg, the bus, the rain,
my mother, my life, my looks.

The old man shuddered upright,
opened his eyes wide and smiled,
waggling the loaf in salute
when he saw his neighbour's child –
erstwhile urchin of the street,
turned lanky, lumpen, self-moiled –
facing him in a dull fret
across the bus-aisle's damp cold.

Yet, who was I to refuse
Mr Greenberg, the baker –
homeward-bound with his bonus
of fresh bread and buns to spare!
He croaked something in Yiddish,
and tossed a bag through the air,
gesturing in emphasis
while I grabbed, lurched, juggled, swore

and slumped back, nursing the catch –
Eccles Cakes warm in my hands.
Woozy: weak with self-reproach
and vague spite, I felt my mind
modifying itself a touch,
towards kindness long disowned;
but I held my sulky slouch,
not wishing to understand.

Then we were both up and off
and out in the drizzling rain,
Mr Greenberg – the long loaf
hidden down his gabardine –
and I, staggering, aloof,
solitary and sullen –
though his friendly arm and laugh
helped me home, my mother's son.

First Date

Our conversation was dull
and dangerous equally,
letting loose a bored malice
that would tie and belie us –
we two, so free and easy
in sweet youth on an Earl's hill.

What are we to make of our
heedless walk and where it led?
Perhaps lies, perhaps poems,
perhaps hopeless, waking dreams
in which we drink our own blood
and beat our breasts in despair.

But you are dead, and don't care
whether talk, walk, an Earl's hill,
or our shared future's glimpsed face,
kindled betrayal and madness –
and how am I to recall
such an occult disaster?

A Cripple

Barrel-chested and deep-voiced,
swinging his short leg nimbly
between old wooden crutches,
Alf Williams swept along
Cheetham Hill Road, on his way
from somewhere to somewhere else.
A bow-tie bobbed at his throat;
he hummed "My Grandfather's Clock",
then "Trees" in a lower key;
when he met ladies he knew,
he stopped to raise his Trilby
and make light conversation.

Why am I picturing him
like this? More often than not
I met him in our kitchen –
crutches propped against the wall,
while he sprawled in the armchair,
drinking tea with my mother.
They had been young together –
playmates in these very streets
long before I was thought of.
Laughter boomed from his big face
as he remembered old times.
My mother's teacup jiggled,
his misshapen boot shifted,
as if seeking some foot-ease
from the threadbare jute matting
rucked on the lumpy, flagged floor –
and I ran in and ran out,
full of immediate life.

By the time I was sixteen
I'd come to dislike his rants
against blacks and foreigners
and his bullying contempt
for the watery-eyed wife
scuttling about to please him
in the impoverished house
I had to visit sometimes
on errands for my mother.
But by then I'd seen pictures
of him in his youthful pride,
clear-eyed above tensed biceps
in a group with my mother's
brothers and my grandfather,
"The Prince Street Gymnasium"
displayed on a painted board
among their Indian Clubs,
long before the First World War.
And when I visited him
in hospital some years on,
he was just a dying man –
youth, age and opinions
lost from mind in the coma
squirting from a morphine pump.

I thought of Alf Williams
this afternoon, as I walked
stiffly uphill from Main Street
on my seventieth birthday –
both the man in my young life
and the man in the poem
awaiting my attention
on the desk in my study.
But, back at my desk, I can't
differentiate between
the real, the imagined

and the byways of word play,
nor am I keen to do so.

Let this dubious tribute
to the man I hardly knew
suffice as memorial –
the only words I can find
to save him from nothingness.

Ignorant Love

I see my sister's right arm
swing over and her wrist flick
as she delivers the ball –
a flighted, fizzing leg-break
that makes the last batsman squirm,
before taking his off-bail.
In the dream, I'm eleven,
so my sister must be ten,
our secret-weapon spinner
whenever she deigns to join
us lads on the uneven
patch of back-alley cinder,
where we play cricket till dark
and after. But in the dream,
it's twilight, our opponents
yelling "No ball!" in the gloom,
my sister smoothing her frock
with dismissive nonchalance
on a perspective of street-
lights just lit, and I gazing
at her in ignorant love,
my keen, fielder's crouch easing,
but troubled by something moot,
like flesh restive to relieve
soreness by shifting in bed –
then I am seventy-four,
aching awake to snow-light
in another country, where
my poor sister is long dead,
a woman I grew to hate.

Things Unsaid

"Now *that's* the style of smart hat
you buy a wife the first time
she learns you've been unfaithful!"
proclaimed my mother-in-law,
pointing a finger like fate
at a hat on a column,
all alone in the middle
of a boutique's bright window.

We newly-weds stood speechless,
beside her in Kensington
High Street, our linked hands
fidgeting whether to part
at her Celtic skittishness,
while "Has she been at the gin?"
flashed through our separate minds,
knowing her secret habit.

This is invention – the scene
is vague in my memory.
A year later she was dead
and her daughter, new mother
to the first of our children.
In life, my mother-in-law
had been a stranger, who said
nothing else I remember,

but soon her voice filled my head
every time I regained sense,
in bed with a strange woman.
Not that her flighty advice,
(the grand gesture, outmoded
even then), served to announce
a balance in transgression –
I didn't put it to use.

For whatever my wife learned
of my blithe adultery
she kept to herself, as if
intent on her own secret,
or on some secret beyond
the marriage she shared with me.
Her mother's and father's life,
perhaps? – that waste of polite

responses and things unsaid
in upper-class English and
Donegal-Irish accents?
There is so much I don't know.
Now – impotent, long-widowed,
ignorantly near my end –
I scrutinize such figments,
hoping wisdom might follow.

At the Artists' Union, 1988

A secretary's name-day:
savouries, cakes and drinks,
easy office bonhomie –
the President smiles and winks.

He's joined in the fun, of course,
as a good boss should;
he did so when times were worse:
betrayals, trials, blood.

Now, it's a writer warned,
a painter criticized,
a politician spurned,
but never victimized.

He beams around the room –
and not in mere pretence
of being free from blame
for earlier offence.

It was the State, the State,
a monstrous evil then,
that frightened kindly habit
from ordinary men!

He makes an office joke,
grateful for better days
in which to be craven-weak,
but harmless among the bays,

in which (though certain looks
slither away from his)
no higher strictures tax
his genial cowardice.

A toast is raised to Friendship,
tumbler on tumbler clinks;
enough of talking shop –
the President smiles and winks.

Then and Now

I used to watch her work,
risking her Goddess-beauty
at sink and cooking-stove.

Again I see her peel
nappies from shit-clogged buttocks,
smiling with lifted nose.

And all for my good glance?
The chance of another poem
shocked into lurching life?

No – she was fully grown
and brimful of kitchen joy,
words that needn't be uttered.

Or not for many years,
until she was dead and gone
and I spoke them at last.

From Cheetham Hill

Our Local Cinema

The Globe had been a tram-shed long before
I first eyed Errol Flynn in *Captain Blood*.
A dirty, draughty, flea-pit, braced and bare,
it looked like nothing *better* than a tram-shed
when feeble lights went up, and the man
who owned the place appeared upon the stage
to beg our patience with the latest breakdown,
(Raspberries, hoots and whistles, yells of rage!)

But in palatial darkness, magic beamed –
across tobacco-clouded, stagnant air –
momentous scenes, foreshortened and bizarre,
that moved above my wide-eyed, upturned face
in the front row: a tilted world undreamed-
of, if you weren't sat in the Tuppennies.

Between Two Wars

My uncle, stepping from his Triumph Gloria,
was all I could conceive of worldly wealth –
a business-suited Titan, poised in grandeur,
from whose mellifluous and smiling mouth
flowed kindly words appropriate to poverty,
from whose hand slipped the timely half-a-crown
whenever he saw fit to visit Dorothy,
his ruined sister with the drudge's frown.

A pat for me, reminder of her ruin
(the no-good husband, gone without a trace)
and then I would skedaddle to examine
that huge machine gleaming outside the house,
while mother and her brother in the kitchen
talked about things they wouldn't to my face.

The World and Its Ways

Mr Mantell, the Lithuanian Jew,
said to me once, "I not a British vorkman;
a British vorkman sit on 'is arse all day;
please, do not call me a 'British vorkman!'"
I was a youth; he a man of sixty,
or thereabouts. I didn't know him well,
but now and then he'd stop me in the street, fix me
with a friendly-furious stare and start to rail
against the world and all its wretched ways –
never pausing to ask me what I thought.
When he was done, he'd sniffle, squeeze his eyes
and curse in Yiddish, suddenly remote.
Sometimes he'd laugh and take me by surprise,
the collar-less collarstud jiggling at his throat.

Homage to Terpsichore

At Professor Chilton's Dance Academy,
a rouged instructress, Mrs Hennessy,
pushed me around the floor to waltzes,
quicksteps, tangos, foxtrots, rumbas,
in a chilly hall on rain-dark evenings
awkward with youth and bad beginnings.
This was my route to the suave, the civil,
before Rock & Roll in a time of Skiffle.

I dreamed of a bronze, or gold medallion –
myself and partner in mystic union,
swaying, gliding and making easy
the Reverse Turn With Syncopated Chassis,
but lessons stumbled on till December,
then slurred to an end I can't remember.

Difficult Days

Poems laud the enemy;
lovers count pennies;
the cat drops dead;
wise men fume and fret.

Arthritis locks my fingers;
old friends prove treacherous;
once-clear thoughts blur;
the news gets worse.

I stay home, homeless;
sitcoms turn ominous;
in the toilet bowl's depths
broods a lunar eclipse.

But authorless emails,
full of spelling mistakes,
promise swift relief
and universal peace.

A Game

The boys I knew
and the boys I didn't,
a ragged crew,
went down to the Crescent.
We took a bat,
a ball, some wickets
and my sister, Pat,
to umpire our efforts.
The pitch was short,
the surface bumpy,
so that our sport
was brief and spunky –
ending in blows
and runs disputed,
a punch on the nose,
a boundary clouted.
Pat declared boys
were silly and savage,
all sweaty noise
and the smell of cabbage.
She tossed her curls
and left in a temper
(so much for girls
when you need an umpire).
Then the boys I knew
and the boys I didn't
agreed that we drew
the match on the Crescent,
and arranged to meet
for a definite clincher
in William Street,
before the winter.

Frost at Sennelager

British Army of the Rhine

Guarding the petrol dump
on a German winter's night
my mate and I stood down
sometime before first light.

The Guardhouse Nissen hut
welcomed us to its womb,
a coke-stove gleamed and smoked
in the warm, fuggy room.

I climbed to the squeaking wires
of a mattress-less bed,
and slept there, fully clothed,
as soon as I lowered my head.

The Guard Commander's voice,
his gravelly, sergeant's "Fuck!"
woke me – I don't know when –
the night outside still black.

The two on-duty guards
stood by the open door
heaving a heap of clothes
they dropped to the guard-room floor,

as I – still in a dream –
watched from my distant place
their hands, their dangling arms,
the sergeant's angry face.

"Where did you find this heap? –
he's either drunk or dead!"
"Near the perimeter wire,"
one of the guards said.

Like something in my dream
wobbling into nightmare,
the clothing upon the floor
sprouted a head of hair,

found sprawling, crooked limbs,
un-creased a louring face
and heaved itself erect,
fixing me with a gaze

whose recognition dawned
like a remembered curse.
"Bastard!" it hissed at me,
"I've been hunting you for years!"

The eyes locked mine, it lurched
slow-motion down the room,
to claim me where I crouched,
transfixed and struck dumb.

The sergeant and the guards
stood tranced in a deep spell –
I glimpsed them far away,
silent and statue-still.

And then the eyes were gone –
that doom-like metaphor
collapsed to muddy clothes,
heaped on the guard-room floor.

The waking world revived;
the guards began to laugh,
the sergeant spat and swore
at some man's blameless gaffe,

and ordered the guards to drag
the heap of clothes from sight,
"Back where you found him first,
the stupid, drunken shite!"

My mate, in the bed below,
snored peacefully on;
I trembled through the springs
at what had come and gone,

and who I was, and why
the quarry looked like me,
and what offence had earned
such occult enmity?

Questions a troubled sleep
asked of my youthful fears,
and asked of middle age –
and asks of seventy years.

Mother and Daughter

Browsing among her dead mother's addresses
she yearns for confirmation from the book –
that catalogue of deaths and other losses.

Between its lines lurk secret loves, caresses
and many beds. She feels a little sick
browsing among her dead mother's addresses.

With shame? With envy? What are those strange flushes
changing her cheeks? Why must she rake and rake
that catalogue of deaths and other losses?

She rises, crosses, sniffs the boudoir roses,
remembering gifts from men. Soon she is back
browsing among her dead mother's addresses.

Whose names mean nothing. Voices, manners, faces
clamped in clay. It's a code she cannot break,
that catalogue of deaths and other losses.

Why does she crave adulterous vows and kisses
of one whose constancy was like a rock,
browsing among her dead mother's addresses –
that catalogue of deaths and other losses?

Annual Visits

i.m. Jack Marriot

Your pub was an ill-lit, toilet-tiled vault,
just across from the graveyard. Full of drinkers
like zombies on a night out.

But that's where you felt at ease – there,
and in the canteen of the nearby mental hospital,
chatting with mates you'd made inside.

Or were you having me on? – like the time
you emigrated to Spain, where it was so bloody hot
you lived in an air-conditioned cinema

until you could get a ticket home?
I never knew what to think. You walked me past
the sewage works, down cinder tracks

to a derelict mill and lonely pond,
whose wrinkling water reminded you of wartime –
you wouldn't tell me how, or why.

Going home, you smiled to yourself,
between the vandalized trees of Prestwich Clough
and through the new council estate.

I thought you must have been pondering wartime,
but then you spoke of a casserole, ready to eat
and waiting for us, back at the house.

Other years, you forgot to shop,
your legs were bad, your Benefit hadn't arrived.
I never stayed long, anyway.

Then it was near-wins on the Pools –
and once you asked my opinion of a poem
you'd found in a drawer, something so old

you couldn't remember when you'd written it.
The poem was mine – pretentious, long disowned.
A secret I sheltered, with faint praise.

2

The flat smack of northern vowels
comes tingling back, as I think of walks
taken with you, of mock quarrels
leading to daft disputes and jokes.

Often we chose the pathway, sunken
beside the mental hospital's wall,
where big trees whispered like women
shocked by behaviour crudely male.

Not mine, not yours; we were the smilers,
the understanders, teachers' pets:
monstrous conceits of lonely mothers
maddened by abandonment and defeats.

So – very polite passing the madhouse,
(familiar wards, obliging staff) –
we talked of ills that didn't shame us,
our blunt evasions good enough.

Then – didn't we reach that ruined valley
with broken buildings, wrecked machines,
a scummed lodge and a solitary
fisherman sleeping beside his lines?

I think so: yes, but you stay silent —
maybe the dead remember nowt
of open vistas and close confinement,
dialect, friendship, feeling, thought?

Or maybe you mean to taunt me stupid,
alone in my right, imagined place,
as if it mattered what I, or you did,
together or not on certain days!

Do I expect a final reckoning:
a "Yes", a "No", or bar-room nod?
What little remains of you is fading
fast down an unadopted road

that leads to your chair beneath the wall-clock,
where muddle, loneliness, dust, despair,
enfold the room in somnolent music,
dying, with you, into silent air.

Oaxaca

for Catherine Hall

Candle-flames bent in the lightly perfumed breeze,
on all the tables that crowded the *plazuella*.
Midnight: the stores were closing; three small boys
tussled and shoved beneath the bougainvillaea.

I thought you spoke, but you said it was someone else,
joking in Swiss, or Dutch, at the next table.
The proprietress served us two more ice-cold Pils,
relying on tourists, but quietly kind and capable.

From nearby streets came horn-honks, drunken shouts,
laughter, music, tire-squeals on the cobbles.
I cocked my ears for sudden pistol shots,
clattering soldiers, slogan-chanting rebels.

You spoke – but I was lost in that backward dream
past cyber-cafés, past hipsters trawling discos;
you nudged me awake – to a girl you couldn't name
who was walking past. A model? – *somebody* famous.

Why not? – the Revolution's wrinkled face
now smiled on market forces, trade agreements
and safe vacations for a travelling class
which fluttered plastic cards to make its payments.

My thoughts went dull. We walked to our hotel.
You talked of possible outings for tomorrow.
Rent push-bikes? Walk to the Virgin's waterfall?
Visit the birthplace of the local hero?

Already we'd clambered to the ancient site
above the town – piled stones and windy spaces.
An afternoon of squabbles best forgot,
where hearts had been ripped from living sacrifices.

Morning at the Astoria, 1976

Breakfast: a hard-boiled egg, a slice of ham,
watched by waiters with nothing else to do,
and four girls, fidgeting for trade to use them,
in a perfume kiosk. I picture the Gestapo,
headquartered here during the Second World War –
punctual, booted, bureaucratic men
reflected in these ormolu-framed mirrors,
striding to and fro as work began.

The cheerful maids cleaning my room upstairs
would have been cleaning theirs, then. I crack
and peel the egg, pondering human fate.
In the residents' lounge, facing a bustling street,
international agreements are being struck
between Arab arms dealers and local whores.

To Sakhalin

*"I want to write about devils, about terrifying
women, about wizards – but, alas! the demand
is for well-intentioned tales."*

A. CHEKHOV TO YE. M. SHAUROVA, 1894

When we reached the hut, nothing moved:
the old man sat dead, the owner.
The stove was long cold; the rest
had gone – you could see their tracks in the snow.

I looked at the forest: it was black, black,
with the baying of beasts within it. The red
sun, huge in the sky, warmed nothing.
The boy coughed: his lips were bloody.

Somewhere beyond the hills prisoners
hugged their rags and cursed God
as they shuffled to work. They didn't know it,
but we were supposed to be bringing food

and clothing and freedom. The boy coughed
again and the old man toppled
from his perch. We carried him out
and heaped snow on the rigid shape.

So that much was done. I spoke seriously
to the bearded guide; he began to protest.
He snapped an inch from his frozen moustache
and asked to go back. He looked flustered.

The boy was haemorrhaging badly; my piles
were itching. I sensed a story,
far back in a warm room in a city,
and wrote an imaginary letter to R.

"Dear R, we will never reach there, I fear.
Werewolves abound. The Tyumen coach
was full of illiterate Tax Collectors.
The inns are awful; the natives wretches!"

I signed it in the boy's blood – he died
before I could diagnose his condition.
The Guide disappeared, leaving a note:
"Sorry, gov'ner, it just ain't worth it."

Fortunately I found the nearest port,
the steamer waiting – a dangerous flirt
expecting me among the passengers.
At least, they served excellent yoghurt.

The homeward voyage was full of surprises;
my piles ached, but that was nothing.
Later I wrote an account of the trek:
fiction, of course; I don't pretend to truth.

A British Visitor's Passport

i.m. F. C.

The photograph shows her face, its dangerous beauty,
in nineteen sixty-six – she must have been thirty.
Three children by then; her mother dead, her father
married again, to a Countess in her splendour.

Her gaze is an actress's: fake, bold, quizzical,
in a self-invented role that is inescapable –
and yet the adventure ahead is of *my* making:
a secret, criminal flight, with her starring.

She'd gone along to the post office with our friend,
who needed a Visitor's Passport – to abscond;
then, seeing his nervous mien, his tottering will,
she'd asked for a passport herself, flashing a smile
of unforgettable brilliance on some clerk
who'd later assist detectives' fumbled work
at hunting us down – for helping our friend skip bail
and flee the country, to save himself from gaol.

Headstrong, willful decisions went with her courage,
nor was this the last drama that marked our marriage –
a partnership strained by daily instability,
disputes about meaning, food, domestic polity.

All balanced now in the final equilibrium
of death: her little life become a poem
made by a man who fumbles with awkward patience
to place a name among the constellations.

Housebound

for Jane Poncia

Dogs are "having relationships"
in the park across the street;
what is there to do but watch them?

She sighs and shifts the foot
propped on the table near her book
and the paper. Should she read
of Balkan wars and actors' lives,
or hobble up to bed?
So much for bunion surgery's charms,
and the convalescent state;
so much for being divorced and sixty
in a rented, one-bedroom flat.

Most dogs are sniffing, two dogs are coupling.
Every owner's alone,
walking obscure, private desires
through low evening sunshine.
Sometimes they turn and call their dogs.

She watches from her window,
sorely tried, sourly amused
in the sodium streetlights' glow.

Mementoes

A pipe-tool, a wristwatch, a plaited belt,
a book of Thomson's prose, a pair
of rabbit-fur gloves, beginning to moult,
and a Czech recording of "Abdelazar"

remind me of old friends, now dead,
remind me as I'd not foreseen –
my waking thoughts inhibited
by what I possess of each man.

Either the widow dried her tears
to say, "He meant you to have *this*,"
or else suggested I choose from treasures,
worthless to her, that were once his.

When I chance upon them about the house –
these things I didn't equate in life
with the men who owned them – I grow querulous,
thinking each pathetic proof

of live affection a stumbling block
to apprehending friends now gone.
There lies the watch, the tool, the book,
obstructive, bland, non-partisan.

I wish I'd not encumbered recall
with such recalcitrant mementoes –
they render remote comrades I still
wish for among my joys and sorrows.

Now, only in dreams do they break bounds,
heedless of personal property
as they were in life – impatient friends,
eager to drink and talk with me.

In a Strange House

"You're a good poet, but not much of a lover,"
she said, lighting a cigarette,
collecting herself primly and turning over
away from me in the double, marriage bed –
while I, not wishing to show my boredom,
blew at the rose tattoo on her shoulder-blade.
She twitched and sighed. "It's not for your want of trying,"
she said, smoke wreathing from hidden lips,
"but still, you fuck without faith – as if you're fleeing
the here-and-now in hope of something else."
I coughed, my eyes on a curtain-cornice.
"Not that *I'm* prime," she said. "For all my wiles
I've trapped myself in a miserable marriage –
why, even this is better than that!
I should ask for a divorce, but haven't the courage."
She flounced onto her back, covered a breast,
and looked at me like a worried sister
in search of advice. I think I was nonplussed,
or did I say some kind words, now forgotten,
or were my thoughts in other rooms
where women smiled, or poems lay part-written?
It was long ago. I know she kissed the hand,
I was trying to zip my faulty fly with,
before she murmured, "Thanks – I'll see you around."

Morning Face

Who can this old man be
staring straight back at me
from out the bathroom mirror?
Surely he comes in error
for somebody bold and young,
ambitious, tightly strung,
nimble with vows and theses,
apologies, women's kisses?

Not so – I know his name
and incontrovertible claim
to represent me fairly,
weekly, monthly, yearly.
His wrinkled gaze is mine,
his heightening forehead's shine,
the secret disgrace he suffered,
the wisdom he never offered.

Yet he resembles men
I liked when I was ten –
curmudgeons, rueful cadgers,
greybeards, decrepit lodgers –
so I wink at these living links;
but the man in the mirror winks
directly at me, insistent
that death's not far distant.

Family Matters

1

Your father – the incorruptible Public Servant
who dined with union leaders, knew the "P.M."
and called the head of Bethlehem Steel "a damn
likeable fellow, for a Yank" – was distant
towards your poet-love with northern vowels.
Until I questioned him on High Finance
and proved myself an economics dunce,
though keen for enlightenment from kindly moguls –
principally him. Then he became expansive,
all dividends, hedging, futures, balanced funds,
technical breakouts, small caps, stocks and bonds –
the flowers of the field where he was active.
But not one question did he ask of me
concerning literature and poetry.

2

Your Aunt Elizabeth lived in genteel poverty,
her Tudor mansion deep in leafy grounds –
one fifteenth-century wing a sometime priory,
where carpets lifted, still, in winter winds.
The aged Smith functioned as butler/chauffeur;
Fortnum & Mason's van came once a week;
an Admiral phoned; a General was a suitor;
Elizabeth smiled and read another book.

Our children loved to visit there, when little,
to be indulged like Royalty by Smith,
who'd call them "Master Simon", Miss Rebecca",
and bring them tea in bed and run a bath.
While great-aunt smiled and fed her corgi cake,
and yawned and smiled and read another book.

3

What of your mother? – never recovered, it seemed,
from marrying an English business gent
against the combined will of her Belfast clan –
she hid her Queen's College science degree
among Kensington chatter. If ever her husband dreamed
she'd play The Hostess, easing his Ascent,
he woke to find half-empty glasses of gin
in every room and Isabel worse than tipsy.

"Mummy's not well" was the burden of a song
echoing through your girlhood, in that flat
full of uneasy claims to upper-class
respectability. You knew something was wrong ...
then Daddy climbed beside you in the night –
and made of your eighteen years a demure fortress.

4

I was about to quit the steady job
I'd held for sixteen years – already a few
good poems written, already the secret nub
of another, better life beginning to show.
You were a new arrival in the North –
glamorous creature with a Mayfair voice
and imperious manner – born to rule the earth,
bearing the radiant stigma of your class.

How we confused each other with our claims
to be what we were, and every claim unspoken;
you slept with many to advance your schemes,
I turned away when most inclined to beckon.
Each glittered in the other's clouded gaze:
danger – a dagger, offered as a prize.

5

You couldn't become a Lassie from Lancashire,
even by flattening vowels, eating tripe
and drinking with the lads. In fact, the endeavour
made you a joke to some you sought to ape
and troubled my thoughts – already running on
knower and known as a Mobius Strip:
the solid world and the imagination
inscribed on the selfsame, seamless loop.

I could believe yours had an extra twist,
or none at all. You'd glow like an honoured guest
in places you had no understanding of;
misread faces, voices; mistake Mine Host
for a fearsome monster met with once in sleep
and make false loves appear by *willing* love.

6

No bank would lend us money on that house –
only the owner, eager to unload it –
and yet its run-down promise suited us,
as did the raffish, noisy streets around it.
You were an almost-mother, at your ease,
placid in your acceptance, but astounded;
I was a Reputation on the Rise,
smiling on talk shows, amiably candid.

We bought the house and settled to our lives,
which weren't the lives we thought we saw beginning:
children, betrayal, madness, early graves,
in short order demanded to know the meaning.
Then waved our mute selves on to a new place,
or newly same, with hints of happiness.

7

You murmured that if you'd not met me,
you'd have married a weak man and made his life
a hell on earth. Speaking light-heartedly –
soothed after novel love as a new wife –
you poked my groin with one raised knee,
and told me I was more than strong enough
to keep in check your latent devilry,
without demanding submissiveness as proof.

Did I believe you then? I don't know,
we both tried out our truths in many styles
and versions that were difficult to follow –
confusion for the unacknowledged souls
we pressed to loving service, foe on foe,
in intimacy's blood-smeared battles.

EKCO Model AD36

That Bakelite box has long-time stood,
like childhood's strangely imagined God,
firm among icons better loved
from which all detail has been removed.

Squat on a shelf that was always loose –
because there was no Man of the House
to nail, or screw, or make a prop –
it brooded over my growing up,

alone in a corner: anchorite,
oracle moved by an inner light,
from whose masked mouth's amazing O
came *Hilversum, Berlin, Zagreb, Moscow,*

and in between, blurred voices, music,
unidentified call-signals and static.
Riddling answers for a fatherless son
who'd yet to put the world to question,

being half-stunned from early trauma –
concussed into believing his mother's
niggardly view of human scope
imprisoned in a local landscape.

With her I listened contentedly
to serials on the BBC,
was pleased by long variety shows,
repeated smug comedians' mottoes,

and changed stations, or switched off,
at programmes not familiar enough
to feed the evening's cosiness
meant to be nourished by the wireless.

As if her mind defined her son's!
As if my solitary devotions
before the set's exalted self,
speaking in tongues upon its shelf,

were sexual dreaming, common sense
would not admit or countenance!
Yet, left alone, free of her rule,
I almost knew the twiddled dial

invoked a spirit capable
of conjuring secret truths from Babel,
and that my soul was listening in
to parables of its origin,

passage, and final happy home,
far from a family living room.
I see myself, a supplicant:
awe-struck, puzzled, ignorant,

kneeling upon the rickety back
of a lumpy sofa – ear stuck
close to the mouth's amazing O
on parentless evenings long ago.

My fingers on the tuner move
with premonitions of agile love.
The oracle speaks; rapt, I adore
all nameless knowledge I am bound for.

Index of Titles